'Surprising, provocative, fun' Tim Harford, author of *The Undercover Economist*

'Are there any nice little books I could buy as a present that wouldn't insult the recipient's intelligence? Yes. Or rather *Yes!*' *Guardian*

'All the tips for getting a "yes" are ... inventive and intriguing' *Independent*

'The book is a treasure trove of information ... *Yes!* is a fascinating read and offers countless insights into the way consumers behave. The perfect Christmas present for any business man or woman' *Business Life*

'Jedi-like ... an entertaining guide to 50 tried and tested methods of persuasion' *Esquire*

'Rather a good read ... earnest and honest' *Evening Standard*

'You should read this book. You should read it because you'll enjoy it; because it's perfectly pitched for smart businesspeople; because it's easy to dip into while waiting for a colleague or a plane; and because if you don't someone else is going to get one over you ... Charmingly practical ... the punchy, eager prose keeps things ticking along' Octavius Black, co-author of *The Mind Gym*

'Entertaining, eye-opening – it's all good stuff and very well presented' *Spiked.com*

'Serves up plenty of weird and wonderful case histories' *Sunday Express*

About the authors

Dr Noah J. Goldstein is a faculty member at the Anderson School of Management at UCLA, California. His scholarly research and writing have been published in many of the premier psychology and business journals, and he has been awarded research fellowships and grants from several US government institutions, including the National Science Foundation and the National Institutes of Health. He has also consulted for a number of corporate and government organisations, including Accenture, the United States Forest Service, and the United States Census Bureau

Steve J. Martin is the Director of Influence At Work (UK). He has a background in sales and marketing and has written numerous articles that have been featured in a variety of business publications and the national press. He is a columnist for the British Airways in-flight magazine *Business Life* and also writes for the Institute of Leadership and Management. He speaks at conferences all over the world and regularly presents on the subject of influence and persuasion at a number of business schools, including Cranfield University and the Cass London Business School.

Dr Robert B. Cialdini is Regents' Professor of Psychology and Marketing at Arizona State University. He is the world's most quoted expert in the field of influence and persuasion and the author of the groundbreaking book *Influence: Science and Practice*, which has sold over one million copies. His research appears in a wide range of academic and business journals and has attracted the attention of businesses and governments alike. In 2003, he was awarded the Donald T. Campbell Award for his distinguished contribution to the field of social psychology.

YES!

50 secrets from the science
of persuasion

Noah J. Goldstein PhD, Steve J. Martin
and Robert B. Cialdini PhD

P

PROFILE BOOKS

For my parents and, of course, for Jenessa – NJG
For my niece and nephew Casie Leigh and Riley – SJM
For my granddaughter Hailey Brooke Cialdini – RBC

First published in Great Britain in 2007 by
Profile Books Ltd
3a Exmouth House
Pine Street
Exmouth Market
London EC1R 0JH
www.profilebooks.com

Copyright © Noah J. Goldstein, Steve J. Martin and Robert B. Cialdini 2007

10 9

The moral right of the authors has been asserted.

All rights reserved. Without limiting the rights under copyright reserved
above, no part of this publication may be reproduced, stored or introduced
into a retrieval system, or transmitted, in any form or by any means
(electronic, mechanical, photocopying, recording or otherwise), without
the prior written permission of both the copyright owner and the publisher
of this book.

A CIP catalogue record for this book is available from the British Library.

ISBN: 978 1 84668 016 8

Text design by Sue Lamble
Typeset by MacGuru Ltd
info@macguru.org.uk

Printed and bound in the UK by CPI Bookmarque, Croydon, CR0 4TD

Mixed Sources
Product group from well-managed
forests and other controlled sources
www.fsc.org Cert no. TT-COC-002227
© 1996 Forest Stewardship Council

Contents

YES!

Introduction

If all the world's a stage, then small changes in your lines can have dramatic effects

There's an old joke that the comedian Henny Youngman would tell about his previous night's accommodation: 'What a hotel! The towels were so big and fluffy that I could hardly close my suitcase.'

Over the last few years, however, the moral dilemma facing hotel guests has changed. These days, the question of whether to *remove* the towels from their room has been replaced by the question of whether or not to *reuse* the towels during the course of their stay. With the increasing adoption by hotels of environmental programmes, more and more travellers are being asked to reuse their towels, to help conserve resources, save energy and reduce the amount of detergent-related pollutants released into the environment. In most cases, this request comes in the form of a card placed in guests' bathrooms.

These cards provide remarkable insights into the often secret science of persuasion.

With a nearly limitless array of angles to play and motivational strings to pull, what words should be put on the card to make the request most persuasive to the hotel guests? Before providing an answer, which we'll do in the first two chapters, let's first ask how the designers of the messages on these little cards typically encourage guests to participate in these programmes. A survey of the messages conveyed by dozens of request cards from a wide variety of hotels around the globe reveals that these cards most commonly attempt to encourage towel recycling efforts by focusing guests almost exclusively on the importance of environmental protection. Guests are almost invariably informed that reusing their towels will conserve natural resources and help spare the environment from further depletion and disruption. This information is often accompanied by eye-catching environment-related pictures, ranging from rainbows to raindrops to rainforests ... to reindeer, even.

This persuasion strategy generally seems to be an effective one. For example, one of the largest manufacturers of these signs reports that most hotel guests who have the chance to take part in these programmes do reuse their towels at least once during their stay. The level of participation produced by these signs can be seen as impressive.

Social psychologists, however, are often on the lookout for ways to apply their scientific knowledge to make policies and practices even more effective. Much like a roadside billboard that reads 'Place your ad here', these little towel recycling cards spoke to us, practically begging us to 'Test your ideas here'. So we did. And, as we'll explain, we showed that by making a small change to the way the request is made, hotel chains can do much, much better.

Of course, how, precisely, one could go about enhancing the effectiveness of these types of environmental campaign is but a single issue. Much more broadly, we're going to claim that everyone's ability to persuade others can be enhanced by learning persuasion strategies that have been scientifically proved to be successful. As this book will reveal, small, easy changes to our messages can make them vastly more persuasive. We will report on dozens of studies, some conducted by us, some by other scientists, that demonstrate this point in many different settings. Along the way, we will discuss the principles behind these findings. Our central purpose is to provide the reader with a better understanding of the psychological processes underlying how we can influence others to move their attitudes or behaviour in a direction that results in positive outcomes for both parties. As well as presenting a variety of effective and ethical persuasion strategies, we discuss the types of things to watch out for to help you resist both subtle and overt influences on your decision-making.

Importantly, rather than relying on pop psychology or the all-too-common 'personal experience', we will discuss the psychology underlying successful social influence strategies in the context of the scientifically rigorous evidence that supports them. We'll do this by pointing towards a number of mystifying occurrences that can be explained by a greater understanding of the psychology of social influence. For example, why, immediately after the news of the passing of one of the most popular popes in modern history, would hordes of people besiege stores some thousand miles away to buy souvenirs that had nothing to do with the pope, the Vatican or the Catholic Church? We'll also provide insights into the single office supply that can make your attempts to persuade others significantly more effective, what Luke Skywalker can teach us about leadership, the mistake communicators often make which causes their message to backfire, how to turn your weaknesses into persuasive strengths, and why sometimes seeing yourself – and being seen by others – as an expert can be so dangerous.

Persuasion as science, not art

Persuasion has been studied scientifically for over half a century now. Yet the research on persuasion is something of a secret science, often lying dormant in the pages of academic journals. Considering the large body of research that's been done on the subject, it might be useful to take a moment to think about why this research is so often overlooked. It's no surprise that people who are faced with choices about how to influence others will often base their decisions on thinking that's grounded in fields such as economics, political science and public policy. What's puzzling, however, is how frequently decision-makers fail to consider established theories and practices in psychology.

One explanation is that, in contrast to how they regard the fields of economics, political science and public policy, which require learning from outsiders to achieve even a minimal level of competence, people believe they already possess an intuitive understanding of psychological principles simply by virtue of living life and interacting with others. As a consequence, they're less likely to learn and to consult the psychological research when making decisions. This overconfidence leads people to miss golden opportunities to influence people – or worse still, to misuse psychological principles to the detriment of themselves and others.

Besides being overly reliant on their personal experiences, people also rely too much on introspection. For example, why would the marketing practitioners commissioned to design the towel reuse signs focus almost exclusively on the impact of these programmes on the environment? They probably did what any of us would do – they asked themselves, 'What would motivate *me* to participate in one of these programmes by recycling my towels?' By examining their own motives, they would realise that a sign that tapped into their values and identity as an environmentally concerned individual would be particularly motivating. But in doing so, they would also fail to realise how they could increase participation just by changing a few words in their request.

Persuasion is a science. It has often been referred to as an art, but this is an error. Although talented artists can certainly be taught skills to harness their natural abilities, the truly remarkable artist depends upon talent and creativity that no instructor can instill in another person. Fortunately, this isn't the case with persuasion. Even people who consider themselves persuasion lightweights – people who feel they couldn't coax a child to play with toys – can learn to become persuasion heavyweights by understanding the psychology of persuasion and by using the strategies that have been scientifically proved to be effective.

Whether you're a manager, a lawyer, a healthcare worker, a policy-maker, a food server, a salesperson, a teacher or something entirely different, this book is designed to help you become a master persuader. We'll describe certain techniques that are based on what one of us (Robert Cialdini) explored in the book *Influence: Science and Practice* as the six universal principles of social influence: reciprocation (we feel obligated to return favours performed for us), authority (we look to experts to show us the way), commitment/consistency (we want to act consistently with our commitments and values), scarcity (the less available the resource, the more we want it), liking (the more we like people, the more we want to say yes to them) and social proof (we look to what others do to guide our behaviour).

We'll discuss what these principles mean and how they operate in some detail, but we won't limit ourselves to them. Although the six principles underpin the majority of successful social influence strategies, there are many persuasion techniques that are based on other psychological factors, which we'll uncover.

We'll also highlight the way these strategies operate in a number of different contexts, focusing not only on the workplace but also on your personal interactions – for example, as a parent, a neighbour or a friend. The advice we'll provide will be practical, action-oriented, ethical and easy to follow, and will require very little additional effort or cost to pay big dividends.

With apologies to Henny Youngman, we fully expect that by the time you finish this book, your persuasion toolbox will be packed with so many scientifically proved social influence strategies that you'll hardly be able to close it.

50

secrets from the science of persuasion

1

How can you increase your persuasiveness by inconveniencing your audience?

Paid programming, in the form of the 'infomercial', is increasingly common on the ever growing number of television channels that are available today. Colleen Szot is one of the most successful writers in the paid programming industry. And for good reason: in addition to penning several well-known 'infomercials' in the USA, she recently authored a programme that shattered a near-twenty-year sales record for a home shopping channel. Although her programmes use many of the elements common to most infomercials, including flashy catchphrases, an unrealistically enthusiastic audience and celebrity endorsements, Szot changed three words in a standard infomercial line which caused a huge increase in the number of people who purchased her product. Even more remarkable, these three words made it clear to potential customers that the process of ordering the product might prove something of a hassle. What were those three words, and how did they send sales through the roof?

Szot changed the all-too-familiar call-to-action line 'Operators are waiting, please call now' to 'If operators are busy, please call again'. On the face of it, the change appears foolhardy. After all, the message seems to suggest that potential customers might have to waste their time dialling and redialling the number until they finally reach a sales representative. That sceptical view, however, ignores the power of the principle of social proof. In brief, when people are uncertain about a course of action, they tend to look outside themselves and to other people around them to guide what they do. In the Colleen Szot example, consider the kind of mental image likely to be generated when you hear 'operators are waiting': scores of bored employees filing their nails or clipping coupons while they wait by their silent telephones – an image indicative of low demand and poor sales.

Now consider how your perception of the popularity of the product would change if you heard the phrase 'if operators are busy, please call again'. Instead of those bored, inactive representatives, you're probably imagining operators going from call to call without a break. In the case of the modified line, home viewers followed their perceptions of others' actions, even though those others were completely anonymous. After all, 'if the phone lines are busy, then other people like me who are also watching this infomercial are calling, too'.

Many classical findings in social psychology demonstrate the power of social proof to influence other people's actions. To take just one, in an experiment conducted by research scientist Stanley Milgram and colleagues, an assistant of the researchers stopped on a busy New York City pavement and gazed skyward for 60 seconds. Most passers-by simply walked around the man without even glancing to see what he was looking at. When the researchers added four more men to that group of sky gazers, however, the number of passers-by who joined them more than quadrupled.

Although there's little doubt that other people's behaviours are a powerful source of social influence, we should point out that when we ask people in our own studies whether other people's behaviour influences their own, they absolutely insist that it does not. But experimental social psychologists know better. We know that people's ability to identify the factors that affect their behaviour is surprisingly poor. Perhaps this is one reason why those in the business of creating those little cards to encourage the reuse of towels didn't think to use the principle of social proof to their advantage. By asking themselves, 'What would motivate *me*?' they might well discount the very real influence that others would have on their behaviour. As a result, they focused all their attention on how reusing the towels would contribute to saving the environment, a motivator that seemed, at least on the surface, to be most relevant to the desired behaviour.

Remember the finding that the majority of hotel guests who encounter the towel reuse signs do actually recycle their towels at least some time during their stay? What if we simply informed guests of this fact? Would it have any influence on their participation in the conservation programme? Two of us and another researcher set out to test whether a towel reuse sign conveying this information might actually be more persuasive than a sign widely adopted throughout the hotel industry.

To do so, we created two such signs and, with the cooperation of a hotel manager, placed them in hotel rooms. One sign was designed to reflect the type of basic environmental protection message adopted throughout much of the hotel industry. It asked the guests to help save the environment and to show their respect for nature by participating in the programme. A second sign utilised the social proof information with the honest message that the majority of guests at the hotel recycled their towels at least once during their stay. These signs, as well as some others we'll discuss later in the book, were randomly assigned to the different rooms in the hotel.

Now, typically, experimental social psychologists are fortunate enough to have a team of eager undergraduate research assistants to help collect the data. But, as you might imagine, neither our research assistants nor the guests would have been very pleased to have the researchers sneaking into hotel bathrooms to collect our data, nor would our university's ethics board (nor our mothers, for that matter). Fortunately, the hotel's room attendants were kind enough to volunteer to collect the data for us. On the first day in which a particular guest's room was serviced, they simply recorded whether or not the guest chose to reuse at least one towel.

When we analysed the data, we found that guests who learned that most other guests had reused their towels (the social proof appeal), which was a message that we've never seen employed by even a single hotel, were 26 per cent more likely than those who saw the basic environmental protection message to recycle their towels. That's a 26 per cent increase in participation relative to the industry standard, which we achieved simply by changing *a few words* on the sign to convey what others were doing. Not a bad improvement based on a factor that people say has no influence on them at all.

These findings show how being mindful of the power of social proof can pay big dividends in your attempts to persuade others. Of course, the importance of the way you communicate this information should not be understated. Your audience is unlikely to respond favourably to a statement like 'Hey, you: be a sheep and join the herd. Baaaaaaaah!' A more positively framed statement like 'Join countless others in helping to save the environment' is likely to be received much more favourably.

Besides the impact on public policy, social proof can have a major impact in your work life. In addition to touting your top-selling products with impressive statistics that convey their popularity (think of the McDonald's sign stating 'Billions and billions served'), you'd do well to remember to always ask for testimonials from satisfied customers and clients. It's also important to feature those testimonials when you're presenting to potential clients who may need reassuring about the benefits that your organisation can provide. Or better yet, you can set up a situation in which your current clients have the opportunity to provide first-hand testimonials to prospective clients about how satisfied they are with you and your company. One way to do this is to invite current and potential customers to a luncheon or seminar and arrange the seating charts so that they can easily mix. In this setting, they're likely to naturally strike up conversations that bring out the advantages of working with your organisation. And if, while taking RSVPs for the luncheon, your potential guests tell you they'll have to call you back to let you know, just be sure to tell them that if your phone line is busy, they should keep trying ...

2

What shifts the bandwagon effect into another gear?

Our social proof message enhanced guests' towel reuse compared with the industry standard, so we know that people are motivated to follow the behaviours of others. But this finding poses another question: *whose* behaviours are people most likely to follow?

For example, would people be more persuaded to reuse their towels by social proof information that conveyed the behaviour of people who previously stayed in *their particular room* as opposed to the hotel in general? There are some good reasons to expect not. In fact, giving greater credence to the norms of your particular room is irrational for two reasons. First, from a purely logical standpoint, it's likely that you won't view the previous occupants of your room in an especially positive light. After all, those are the same people who have, just by staying there previously, played a larger role in reducing the quality of your room and its amenities than any other guests in the hotel. Second, there's no reason to believe that the behaviours of those previously occupying your room are any more valid than, say, the behaviours of those who stayed next door. Yet, as we discussed earlier, much psychological research shows how people are often wrong about what motivates them to engage in certain behaviour.

If you recall, the social proof message used in the hotel study informed guests that others like themselves – specifically, the majority of other guests who had previously stayed at the hotel – had reused their towels at least once during their stay. We decided to take the perceived similarity one step farther by conducting another study in which some hotel guests saw a request to reuse their towels communicating the social proof of guests who had stayed in the *same room* in which they were staying. So, in addition to the standard environmental protection appeal and the social proof appeal used in the prior study, some guests saw a sign informing them that most of the people who had previously stayed in their particular room participated in the towel reuse programme at some point during their stay.

When we analysed the data, we saw that guests who learned that the majority of others in their particular room had participated were even more likely to participate than guests who learned the norms for the hotel in general. And compared to the standard environmental appeal, there was a 33 per cent increase in participation. These results suggest that if Henny Youngman had encountered a sign in his bathroom indicating that not a single person who had previously stayed in his particular room had ever stolen a towel, he probably would have had a much easier time closing his suitcase as he prepared to check out. But why?

It's usually beneficial for us to follow the behavioural norms associated with the particular environment, situation or circumstances that most closely match our own. For example, when you're at a public library, do you follow the norms of other library patrons, quietly browsing through the fiction section and occasionally whispering to your friends, or do you follow the norms of the patrons at your favourite bar, crushing books against your forehead for a dare and playing games where you take a drink every time you read a word with the letter 'e'? If you want to avoid the lifetime ban from the premises that you'd get if the librarian caught you trying to crush that book against your forehead, you'd obviously choose the former rather than the latter.

Earlier, we described the importance of testimonials in trying to sway others' opinions in your direction. The results of this experiment suggest that the more similar the person giving the testimonial is to the new target audience, the more persuasive the message becomes. This means that in deciding which testimonials to show to a prospect, you need to take your ego out of the process. You should begin not with the one you're most proud of, but with the one whose circumstances are closest to those of your audience. For instance, a schoolteacher trying to convince a student to come to class more often should solicit comments about the benefits of doing so not from students in the front row, but rather from students who are more similar to the target student.

As another example, if you are selling software to the owner of a string of local beauty salons, she'll be more influenced by information about how pleased other salon owners are with your software than she will by similar information about the big shots at British Airways. After all, she's likely to think, 'If others *like me* have got good results with this product, then it should be right for me, too.'

And if you're a leader or a manager attempting to persuade employees to embrace a new system, you should ask for a testimonial from others within the same department who have already agreed to make the switch. But what if you've tried that, yet you still have one stubborn employee – perhaps the person who has been working with the older system the longest – whom you still can't win over? A common mistake managers

might make in such a case would be to choose the most elo-
quent co-worker to try to explain the benefits to his or her stubborn colleague, even if he or she is completely different from
that person in a number of important ways. Instead, the manager's best bet would probably be to solicit the opinions of a
similar co-worker – perhaps someone else who had also been
working under the system for a long time – even if that person
happened to be somewhat less articulate or popular.

3

What common mistake causes messages to self-destruct?

Advertisements are typically designed to move products, not people. But in the early 1970s the Keep America Beautiful Organisation created an advertisement that was widely thought to be so moving that many consider it to be perhaps the most effective public service announcement of all time. Designed to infuse America's daily television viewing diet with an extra serving of moral fibre, the spot featured a Native American reacting to the widespread corruption of the environment that he observed by shedding a single but powerful tear. Many years later, the same organisation revisited their old friend in a new campaign. This time, the camera featured several people waiting at a bus stop, doing everyday things such as drinking coffee, reading the newspaper and smoking cigarettes. The bus arrived, they all climbed aboard, and the camera cut to the empty waiting area, now covered with cups, newspapers and cigarette butts. As the camera panned from right to left, it slowly zoomed in on a poster of the Native American overlooking the scene, still with a tear in his eye. As the screen faded to black, the text of the spot's take-home message appeared: 'Back by popular neglect.'

Back by *popular* neglect. What sort of message is conveyed by this phrase and by the environments featured in this advertisement? It tells the viewer that despite strong disapproval of littering behaviour, many people do in fact engage in it. Although communicating strong disapproval of such behaviour might certainly prove motivating, conveying the idea that it is common practice provides strong social proof for engaging in that very behaviour. Because the principle of social proof states that people tend to follow the most popular course of action, it can have harmful effects as well as helpful ones.

Other examples are abundant in everyday life. Health centres and hospitals place posters on waiting-room walls decrying the numbers of patients who don't turn up for their appointments and get frustrated when the non-attendance rates subsequently rise further. Political parties misunderstand the impact of their communications by condemning the rise in voter apathy only to watch as more and more voters fail to turn up to the polls. In Arizona, visitors to the state's Petrified Forest National Park quickly learn from prominent signage that the park's existence is threatened because so many visitors have been taking pieces of petrified wood from the grounds: *'Your heritage is being vandalised every day by theft losses of petrified wood of 14 tons a year, mostly a small piece at a time.'*

Although these instances may indeed reflect reality and clearly stem from the best of intentions, practitioners behind these campaigns may fail to realise that by using negative social proof as part of a rallying cry, they might be inadvertently focusing the audience on the prevalence, rather than the undesirability, of that behaviour. In fact, we became aware of the wood theft problem at the Petrified Forest through a story that a former graduate student told. He had visited the Petrified Forest with his fiancée – a woman he described as the most honest person he'd ever known, someone who had never borrowed a paper clip without returning it. They encountered the park sign warning visitors against stealing petrified wood. While still reading the sign, he was shocked when his otherwise wholly law-abiding fiancée nudged him in the side with her elbow and whispered, 'We'd better get ours now.'

To test the role of negative social proof (and to see whether we could design a more effective message), one of us, along with a team of other behavioural scientists, created two signs designed to deter wood theft at Petrified Forest National Park. The negative social proof sign conveyed the message that many other visitors had stolen wood. It said, 'Many past visitors have removed the petrified wood from the park, changing the natural state of the Petrified Forest,' and was accompanied by a picture of several park visitors taking pieces of wood. A second sign conveyed no social proof information. Rather, it simply stated that stealing wood was not appropriate or approved, saying, 'Please don't remove the petrified wood from the park, in order to preserve the natural state of the Petrified Forest.' That sign was accompanied by a picture of a lone visitor stealing a piece of wood, with a red circle and bar (i.e. the universal 'No' symbol) superimposed over his hand. We also had a control condition in which we didn't put up either of these signs.

Unbeknown to park visitors, we placed marked pieces of petrified wood along visitor pathways. We also varied what sign (if any) was posted at the entrance of each pathway. Through this procedure, we were able to observe how the different signs affected theft.

In a finding that should petrify the National Park's management, compared with a no-sign control condition in which 2.92 per cent of the pieces were stolen, the negative social proof message resulted in *more* theft (7.92 per cent). In essence, it almost tripled theft. This was not a crime prevention strategy; it was a *crime promotion strategy*. In contrast, the other message, which simply asked visitors not to steal the wood, resulted in slightly less theft (1.67 per cent) than the control condition. These results are consistent with the idea that when the social proof for a situation indicates that an undesirable behaviour occurs with regrettably high frequency, it might indeed cause unintentional damage to publicise this information. So, rather than conveying the negative social proof information, communicators in these types of circumstances should focus the audience on what kind of behaviour should or shouldn't be practised in that setting. Or, if the circumstances allow for it, one can focus the audience on all the people who do engage in the positive behaviour. Sometimes, this can be done through simple reframing of the statistics. For example, although 14 tons of wood are stolen each year at the park, the actual number of thieves is minuscule (only 2.92 per cent of the visitor total) compared to the massive number of people who respect the park's rules and choose to preserve its natural resources.

What are the implications for your attempts to be more persuasive? Let's imagine you are a manager recognising that attendance at your monthly meetings has gone down. Rather than calling attention to the fact that so many people are absent, you could not only express your disapproval but also highlight the fact that those who don't attend are in the minority by pointing out the large number of people who do actually turn up. Similarly, business leaders would be well advised to publish the number of departments, employees and/or colleagues that have already incorporated a new way of working, a new software system or a new customer service plan into their everyday procedures. In doing so, they can be assured that they are harnessing the power of social proof as opposed to having it potentially backfire on them by complaining of those who haven't come on board.

4

When persuasion might backfire, how do you avoid the 'magnetic middle'?

The Petrified Forest study makes it clear that people have a natural tendency to do what most other people are doing, even when that behaviour is socially undesirable. But although we recommended trying to reframe the message to focus on all the people who are behaving in a more desirable way in such cases, unfortunately that's not always possible. What's a persuader to do in those situations?

Consider a study two of us conducted with lead researcher Wes Schultz and several other colleagues. First, we obtained permission from around three hundred California households to record their weekly energy use. We then had research assistants go to the sides or backyards of participating homes and read their energy meters to get a baseline measure of how much energy the households consumed per week.* After this, we hung a little card on the front door of each household that gave feedback to the homeowners about how their energy consumption compared to the neighbourhood average. Of course, half of the households consumed more energy

---

* For those concerned for the health of our meter readers, we should note that they performed the task during daylight hours and we didn't allow them to go into backyards with unchained dogs. So rest assured, no assistants were harmed in the making of this research.

than the average, whereas the other half consumed less.

We found that over the next several weeks, those who had been consuming more energy than their neighbours reduced their energy consumption, by 5.7 per cent. Not much of a surprise there. More interesting, however, was the finding that those who had been consuming *less* energy than their neighbours actually *increased* their energy consumption by 8.6 per cent. These results show that what most others are doing acts as something of a 'magnetic middle', meaning that people who deviate from the average tend to be drawn towards it – they change their actions to be more in line with the norm regardless of whether they were previously behaving in a socially desirable or undesirable way.

So, how do we prevent the backfire effect that occurs when people already acting in a socially conscious way learn that they're deviating from the (less desirable) norm? Perhaps it would be helpful to display a small emblem symbolic of society's approval for their positive behaviour, which would not only signal its social desirability but also give positive reinforcement in the form of an ego boost. But what kind of symbol should we use? A thumbs-up image? An actual stamp of approval?

How about a simple smiley face? To test this idea, we included another experimental condition in our study. For these households, the feedback on the card was accompanied by either a smiley face (☺) or a frowny one (☹), depending, of course, on whether they were using more or less energy than the neighbourhood average. The data revealed that the addition of the frowny face didn't make much difference. In other words, those who used a relatively large amount of electricity reduced their consumption by over 5 per cent regardless of whether the feedback included the frowny face. We were impressed, however, by the impact of adding the smiley face to the feedback given to those who used a relatively small amount of electricity. Whereas their no-symbol peers had shown that 8.6 per cent increase in energy consumption that we described earlier, these 'smiley-faced' households continued to consume energy at the low pre-feedback rate.

The results of this study not only demonstrate the power of the social norm to draw people's behaviours towards it like a magnet, but also show how we can reduce the likelihood of our message of approval for desirable behaviour backfiring on the half of the population that receives it.

To take another example, suppose an internal report of a large company becomes public, and it states that the average employee arrives late for work 5.3 per cent of the time. The good news is that those who arrive late more often than that will probably adjust their behaviour to be more in line with the norm, but the bad news is that so will those who are much more consistently punctual. This research makes it clear that those who tend to come in on time should be immediately applauded for their positive behaviour and have it made clear to them how much punctuality is appreciated.

Those who work in public services should also consider the impact of their messages. For example, although there may be rising rates of truancy in classrooms, education personnel should publicly declare the fact that the majority of parents see to it that their children do attend classes regularly, and applaud it, while also showing clear disapproval for the small number of parents who don't.

5

When does offering people more make them want less?

We all know the feeling. We start a new job, and immediately we're inundated with loads of paperwork asking us to make all kinds of important decisions. For many people, just one of those decisions is whether or not to enrol in a retirement plan, in which part of our salary is automatically placed in an invest-ment fund that we'll be able to access later in life. If we decide to enrol, we're typically given many options so that we can find the one that's right for us. Despite the numerous incentives for enrolling in these programmes, however, which often include tax advantages and matching employer contributions, many people don't take advantage of them. Why not? Could it be that organisations are unknowingly discouraging enrolment by offering *too many* options?

Behavioural scientist Sheena Iyengar thinks so. She and several colleagues analysed company-sponsored retirement pro-grammes for nearly 800,000 workers, looking at how the partici-pation rates varied as a function of the number of fund choices offered. Sure enough, the researchers found that the more choices that were offered, the less likely the employees were to enrol in the programme at all. They also found that for every ten additional funds a company offered to its employees, the participation rate dropped almost 2 per cent. To give just one comparison, they found that when only two funds were offered, the rate of participation was roughly 75 per cent, but when 59 funds were offered, the rate dropped to about 60 per cent.

Iyengar and fellow social scientist Mark Lepper also examined whether the damaging effect of offering too much choice held true in other domains, such as food products. They set up a display at an upscale supermarket in which passers-by could sample a variety of jams that were all made by a single manufacturer. Throughout the study, the researchers varied the number of flavours of the jam offered, so that either six or 24 flavours were featured in the display at any given time. The results demonstrated a clear and astonishing difference between the two conditions: only 3 per cent of those who approached the extensive-choice display actually purchased any jam. Contrast that with the 30 per cent who bought jam from the limited-choice display.

What could possibly account for this tenfold increase in sales? The researchers suggest that when so many choices are made available, consumers may find the decision-making process frustrating, owing perhaps to the burden of having to differentiate so many options. This may result in disengagement from the task at hand, leading to an overall reduction in motivation and interest in the product as a whole. The same logic goes for retirement plans.

Does this mean that offering many varieties and alternatives is always a bad thing? Before trying to answer this question, let's first consider one of Vancouver's most celebrated sweet shops, La Casa Gelato. This business offers gelato, ice cream, and *sorbetto* in any flavour you could possibly think of – and many that you couldn't. What began as a Sports and Pizza Bar in the Commercial District of Vancouver in 1982 has grown into what owner Vince Misceo describes as an 'ice cream wonderland'. Upon entering the shop, customers are faced with an eclectic array of over two hundred flavours, including wild asparagus, fig and almond, aged balsamic vinegar, jalapeno, garlic, rosemary, dandelion, and curry, to name only a few.

But considering the research findings we discussed, has Vince Misceo and his shop of over two hundred varieties made a mistake by offering so many choices? The store's proprietor obviously embraces the philosophy that providing his customers with more choices will lead to better business, and it appears from his success that he's right. For one thing, the extensive variety of flavours has generated great publicity for his business – the extremely varied offerings have become a unique, identifying feature of the brand. Second, most of his shop's clientele seem to genuinely savour – both literally and figuratively – the process of sampling and eventually choosing the flavours they would like to try. And third, maximising the number of options available may be especially helpful when customers are likely to know exactly what they want and are simply looking for a shop or a business that supplies it.

However, there are few companies that find themselves in the fortunate position of having hordes of prospective buyers literally salivating at the opportunity to choose from their wide range of goods and services. Instead, it's often the case that potential customers don't know precisely what they want until they've surveyed what's available to them. What this means for most businesses is that by saturating the market with a large number of unnecessary varieties of their products, they could well be inadvertently harming their sales, and as a result diminishing their profits. In such cases, a business might enhance a customer's motivation to purchase its goods and services by reviewing its product line and cutting out redundant or less popular items.

There are a number of major manufacturers of a variety of consumer products that in recent years have been streamlining the range of options they provide, sometimes in response to a modest rebellion by clients against the excessive choices they were offered. For example, take Procter & Gamble, who offer a wide range of products, from laundry detergents to prescription drugs. When the company reduced the number of versions of Head & Shoulders, one of its very popular shampoos, from a staggering 26 to 'only' 15, they quickly experienced a 10 per cent increase in sales.

So what might this mean for you? Suppose that you work for an organisation that sells many varieties of one product. Although it may seem against your intuition at first, it may be worth considering a reduction in the number of options provided by your business in order to drum up maximum interest in your offerings. This could be especially true if you have clients who are uncertain of exactly what they want. Of course, there could be additional benefits of offering less, such as more storage space, reduced spending on raw materials, and a reduction in the marketing and point-of-sale materials needed to support a smaller portfolio. A worthwhile exercise would be to review the extent of your product range and ask yourself the question: Where we have customers who may not be clear about their requirements, might the number of choices we offer be causing them to seek alternatives elsewhere?

The lessons of this research can also be applied to home life. Giving children choices in what books they'd like to read or what dinner they'd like to eat can undoubtedly be beneficial, but too many choices may be overwhelming and ultimately demotivating. The old saying may well assert that variety is the spice of life, but as the scientific research demonstrates, in some circumstances too much variety, like too much spice, can be the ingredient that spoils the dish and, as a result, spoils your efforts to persuade.

6

When does a bonus become an onus?

A stationery set. A ballpoint pen. A cosmetic case. A box of chocolates. A sample vial of perfume or cologne. An oil change. These are all examples of free gifts or services offered by companies, and at some point in your life as a consumer, you've probably been attracted to deals that offer products like these as free gifts with your purchase of another product. Sometimes these little extras can be just the thing to push you to choose one company's product over another. But if everyone likes a free gift, how could it be that giving them can actually backfire?

Social scientist Priya Raghubir wanted to test the idea that when consumers are offered a bonus gift for purchasing a product (the target product), the perceived value and desirability of the bonus gift as a stand-alone product can sharply decline. She suggested that this could be the case because consumers may infer that the product's manufacturer wouldn't give away something valuable for nothing. In fact, it may even lead them to ask, 'What could be wrong with this thing?' People may assume, for example, that the free gift is obsolete or outmoded, or perhaps that the supply overwhelmingly exceeded the demand and the manufacturer is simply trying to purge its inventory.

To test the idea that the value of an item declines when it's offered as a free gift, Raghubir had participants view a duty-free catalogue that featured liquor as the target product and a pearl bracelet as the bonus gift. One group of participants was asked to evaluate the desirability and value of the pearl bracelet in the context of the free gift, and another group was asked to evaluate the pearl bracelet by itself. The results confirmed the hypothesis: people were willing to pay around 35 per cent less for the pearl bracelet when they saw it bundled with the target product as an add-on than when they saw it as a stand-alone product.

These findings reveal some potentially negative consequences for businesses that promote a particular line of products by throwing in goods or services for nothing that the business normally sells independently. Raghubir suggests that one potential way to prevent the gifts or services we offer from boomeranging is to inform or remind customers about the true value of the gift. For example, imagine that you work for a software company. One way that you attract new business is to offer a free piece of software, let's say a security program, to new customers. If in your advertising and your mailings you offer this free product and fail to point out what it would cost customers if they had to pay for it themselves, you are losing out on an effective way of positioning your offer as valuable and significant. After all, if you write down 'free', numerically it is £0.00 – not a message you would want to send to prospective new customers about the worth of your products. To ensure that your offer is seen as the valuable proposition it actually is, the customer needs to be shown its true value. So, no longer should your message read 'Receive a free security program'. Instead, it should become 'Receive a £150 security program at no cost to you'.

The idea of valuing what you do doesn't just apply to those running a business. There are applications for anyone looking to influence others. You might point out to a colleague that you are happy to stay for an extra hour at work to help finish an important proposal because you know how much it means to his or her business prospects. You are valuing your time in your colleague's eyes, a strategy that should prove more influential than simply saying nothing.

Similarly, if you are on the board of a school that's promoting a free after-school club for students, you should point out in the communication to parents what it would cost if they chose a private after-school club instead. In doing this, you would not only create a value for your offering but also probably increase the club's uptake of members as a consequence.

Not only do these findings have implications for business and public service transactions; they might work on your family as well. Perhaps you could use the results of this research to convince your in-laws that, in order to avoid having their opinions devalued, they should stop giving you free advice.

7

How can a new superior product mean more sales of an inferior one?

Some years ago, an American kitchen retail store, Williams-Sonoma, started to offer a bread-making machine that was far superior to the bestselling bread-maker that they stocked. Yet when they added this new product to their inventory, sales of their existing bestseller nearly doubled. Why?

Williams-Sonoma is a hugely successful retail corporation. Its success story started during the late 1940s and early '50s, when a man named Chuck Williams, who worked as a contractor in Sonoma, California, travelled with a couple of his friends to Paris. There, they saw for the first time specialised French cooking equipment – omelette pans and soufflé moulds whose quality and style he'd never seen before in the United States. *Voilà*, the Williams-Sonoma Kitchen Outlet was born. It grew quickly, opening more stores and starting a catalogue business. Today, the company and its subsidiaries have annual retail sales that exceed $3.5 billion. A proportion of these sales come from a bread-maker whose sales nearly doubled immediately after an improved, more expensive one was introduced.

Why? According to researcher Itamar Simonson, when consumers consider a set of choices for a product, they may tend to favour alternatives that are 'compromise choices' – ones that fall between what they need, at a minimum, and what they could possibly spend, at a maximum. When buyers must decide between two products, they often compromise by opting for the less expensive version. If a third product were to be offered that was more expensive than the other two choices, however, the compromise choice would shift from the economy-priced product to the moderately priced product. In the case of the Williams-Sonoma bread-makers, the introduction of a more expensive machine made the original bread-maker seem like a wiser, more economical choice in comparison.

How can lessons learned from a bread-maker leave us, so to speak, rolling in the dough and rising to the occasion? Let's say that you are a business owner or sales manager who has responsibility for the sale of a range of products and services. You would be well advised to recognise that your company's highest-end and highest-priced products provide two very important potential benefits for your business. The first is that these superior products could meet the needs of a small group of current and prospective customers who are attracted to such offerings. As a result, you'll see greater revenues injected into your business by offering them. A second, less obvious and perhaps under-recognised benefit of having a line-up that includes a very high-end version of a product is that the next-highest-priced model is more likely to be considered attractively priced.

Let's take an everyday example where this principle is often not used to its full potential, an example that many of us will be familiar with – choosing a bottle of wine in a bar or restaurant. A substantial number of wine bars and hotels will present their more expensive wines at the bottom of the wine list, which customers' eyes sometimes never get to as they consider the options. In some establishments, the high-end champagnes may even be listed on a separate menu, and as a result the mid-range wines and champagnes aren't presented as compromise choices and therefore could appear less attractive to customers. By simply making a small change and offering these high-end wines and champagnes at the top of their menus, the restaurant or bar will bring to bear the powerful element of compromise.

This strategy can also be effective with work relationships. For example, suppose your organisation decided to pay for you to attend a conference taking place on a cruise ship, and you wanted to stay in a cabin with a window. Rather than simply asking your manager his or her opinion about the window cabin, you can bookend that choice with two other possibilities – one that's not as nice (a windowless inside cabin) and one that's clearly better but perhaps too expensive (a cabin with a balcony). By constructing this set of alternatives around your favourite option, you increase the likelihood that he or she will go for the option you prefer.

The compromise strategy doesn't just apply to bread-makers, alcohol and accommodation. Anyone who has a range of products or services to offer could find their mid-range products becoming more popular by offering more expensive ones first. It's also important to recognise that if your company does employ this high-end framing approach, it could be that an unexpected slump in sales of the highest-end version of a product might tempt you to stop offering it. As this research suggests, however, removing it without replacing it with another top-of-the-line product could produce a negative domino effect that would start with your next-highest-end version of your product and detrimentally work its way down. Such a shift in your customers' compromise choice could land you in a compromising position of your own.

8
Does fear persuade or does it paralyse?

In his first inaugural address, the 32nd US president, Franklin Delano Roosevelt, uttered the following famous words to anxious, Depression-era Americans: 'So, first of all, let me assert my firm belief that the only thing we have to fear is fear itself ... which paralyses needed efforts to convert retreat into advance.' But was Roosevelt correct? When attempting to persuade an audience, does fear paralyse, as he suggested, or does it motivate?

For the most part, research has demonstrated that fear-arousing communications usually stimulate recipients to take actions to reduce the threat. This general rule has one important exception, however: when the fear-producing message describes danger but the recipients are not told of clear, specific, effective means of reducing the danger, they may deal with the fear by 'blocking out' the message or denying that it applies to them. As a consequence, they may indeed be paralysed into taking no action at all.

In one study conducted by Howard Leventhal and colleagues, students read a public health pamphlet detailing the dangers of tetanus infection. The pamphlet was either filled or not filled with frightening images of the consequences of contracting tetanus. In addition, the students either did or did not receive a specific plan for arranging a tetanus injection. Finally there was a control group of students who did not get a warning about tetanus but did get a plan for how to get a tetanus injection. The high-fear message motivated recipients to get a tetanus injection only if it included a plan identifying the specific actions they could take to secure a tetanus injection and thereby reducing their fear of tetanus. This finding helps explain why it's important to accompany high-fear messages with specific recommendations for actions that will reduce the danger: the more clearly people see behavioural means of ridding themselves of the fear, the less they will need to resort to psychological means such as denial.

These findings can be applied to business and beyond. For example, advertising campaigns that inform potential customers of the threats that your company's goods or services can alleviate should always be accompanied by clear, specific and effective steps they can take to reduce the danger. Simply scaremongering customers into believing that your product or service can help with a potential problem might have the opposite effect, cementing them into inaction.

Another implication of this research is that if you happen to spot a particularly serious problem in a large-scale project undertaken by your organisation, you would be wise to accompany your statements to management with at least one plan of action the organisation could take to avert the possible disaster. If you decide that you will tell management first and then generate a plan later, by the time you and your co-workers have developed a plan, management may have already found ways to block out the message or refuse to admit that it applies to that particular project.

Healthcare professionals and public service communicators should be particularly aware of the implications of this study. A physician or nurse who wishes to persuade an overweight patient to lose weight and exercise more should focus that patient on the potential dangers of failing to lose weight, but only if they then follow up that message with some clear, straightforward steps the patient can take to do so – perhaps in the form of a specific diet and a set of exercises. Simply pointing out that they are at an increased risk of cardiovascular disease and diabetes if they do not lose weight might serve only to instil fear and denial in a patient. In the case of public service officials, merely painting a gruesome picture of the impact of dangerous behaviours, such as smoking, having unprotected sex and drunk driving, may also be ineffective – or even backfire – if unaccompanied by a good plan of action.

Given the necessity of pairing a message conveying the potential threat with a clear, specific and easy-to-follow plan, perhaps Roosevelt's statement should be amended to read 'the only thing we have to fear is fear *by* itself'.

9

What can chess teach us about making persuasive moves?

In April 2005, despite facing strong censure by the United States government, the parliament of a sovereign nation voted overwhelmingly to grant citizenship to the former world chess champion and fugitive from US law enforcement Bobby Fischer. What country would risk straining its relationship with the world's most powerful nation to protect an eccentric outlaw who openly speaks highly of the 11 September 2001 hijackers? Was it Iran? Syria, perhaps? How about North Korea?

In fact it was none of these countries. The country whose parliament unanimously voted to grant Fischer citizenship was the nation of Iceland, typically a loyal ally of the United States. Of all the countries in the world, why would Iceland be so willing to welcome Bobby Fischer with open arms, especially after he violated United Nations sanctions by playing a $5 million chess match in the former Yugoslavia?

The answer to this question requires us to go back over thirty years to a very high-profile chess match – the 1972 World Chess Championship match between challenger Fischer and the defending champion, the Russian master Boris Spassky. No match in the history of the game had received more worldwide publicity, and the game of chess was given a tremendous impetus everywhere. The match, played at the height of the cold war, has been dubbed as the Chess Match of the Century.

With typical eccentricity, Fischer failed to arrive in Iceland for the opening ceremony. For several days, it looked doubtful that the match would be played at all, for it was proving impossible for the authorities to accommodate Fischer's myriad of demands, such as banning television cameras and his call for a 30 per cent share of the revenue from spectators. Fischer's behaviour was full of contradictions, as it had been throughout his chess career and his personal life. Finally, after a surprise doubling of the prize fund and a great deal of persuasion, including a reputed phone call from then US Secretary of State Henry Kissinger, Bobby Fischer did fly to Iceland – and went on to beat Spassky handily. By the time the contest had been completed, its coverage had been all over the pages of newspapers both domestic and abroad. In fact, Iceland was willing to tolerate Fischer's controversial persona because, in the words of one Icelandic news reporter, 'he put Iceland on the international map'.

This was apparently seen as a significant gift that Fischer bestowed upon the isolated nation. Such was its significance that, over thirty years later, Icelanders had not forgotten. For instance, a representative in Iceland's foreign affairs ministry made a statement saying that Fischer 'contributed to a rather special event here, over thirty years ago but that people remember very well'. According to the BBC's analysis, Icelanders were 'keen to repay the favour by offering sanctuary to Mr Fischer', even though many people consider Fischer to be unlikable.

This event emphasises the importance and universality of the norm of reciprocity, which obligates us to repay others for what we have received from them. The norm drives us towards fairness in our everyday social interactions, our business dealings and our close relationships, and it helps us build trust with others.

Researcher Dennis Regan conducted a classic study of the reciprocation norm. In the experiment, people who received a small, unsolicited gift from a stranger named Joe in the form of a can of Coca-Cola purchased twice as many raffle tickets from him as those who received no gift at all. This occurred despite the facts that there was a time delay between the gift and the request, and that Joe didn't make any kind of reference to the original gift when he made his pitch about the raffle tickets.

Another aspect of Regan's study sheds some light on why the government of Iceland felt obligated to reciprocate what Fischer had done for the country even though he is such a controversial figure. Interestingly, despite all that has been recorded about the typically strong association between liking and compliance, Regan found that those who received a can of Coke from Joe made their purchase decisions completely irrespective of the extent to which they liked him. In other words, of the participants who had received the gift, those who didn't like Joe purchased just as many raffle tickets as those who did. This demonstrates that the feelings of indebtedness caused by the power of reciprocity are capable of trumping the effects of liking. The fact that the norm of reciprocity has real staying power and transcends liking is insightful for anyone looking to be more persuasive. It should also be welcome news to a person who is asked to do a large or costly favour for another person, for which there appears to be no short-term gain in sight. As informed and ethical influencers, we would be well advised to help out others or make concessions to them first. If we seek out and give our help to a team member, colleague or acquaintance, we have instilled a social obligation for them to help us or support us in the future. Offering help to our boss puts us in a cooperative light in his or her eyes that could serve us well when we need assistance. And the manager who offers to allow a member of his or her staff to leave the office a little early for a dentist's appointment is a manager who has wisely invested in a colleague who will feel the need to reciprocate that gesture and perhaps offer to stay late some time in the future if an important project needs to be completed.

We often make the mistake when we need to persuade and influence others to help us of asking ourselves 'who can help me here?' This may be a short-sighted approach to influencing others. We suggest that it would be more productive to ask ourselves the question 'whom can I help?', knowing that the norm of reciprocation and the social obligation it confers on others will make future requests more effective. If management is about getting things done through others, then a healthy web of indebted colleagues, who have benefited from useful information, concessions and perhaps a friendly listening ear, can stand a manager in good stead for the future. Similarly our friends, neighbours, partners and even children will potentially become more responsive to our requests when we have first provided for them.

We should also note that there's one particular type of person for whom a little favour goes a long way – customer service agents. If you've ever had an incorrect charge on your credit card, tried to make a last-minute change to a plane ticket or wanted to return something, you've probably encountered a less-than-helpful customer service agent at one point or another. To reduce the likelihood that you'll have such an encounter, try the following: if you find towards the beginning of your interaction that the customer service agent is being particularly friendly, polite or responsive – perhaps before you get to your toughest request – tell the agent that you're so happy with the service so far that you're going to write a positive letter or e-mail about your interaction to his or her supervisor as soon as you get off the phone. After getting the agent's name as well as the supervisor's contact information, you can then get to the more complex issues at hand. (Alternatively, tell the person that you're so happy with the service that you'd like to be transferred to the agent's supervisor when you are done so that you can pay the person a compliment.) Although there are several psychological reasons why this might be an effective strategy, the norm of reciprocity is a powerful factor here: you've offered to do a favour for that person, so now that person is going to feel obligated to return the favour. And, for the low cost of writing a quick e-mail to the supervisor afterwards, you can avoid getting into a strategic chess match (and perhaps a screaming match) with the agent that ultimately may lead to disappointment and frustration. So long as you follow through with your promise, the strategy should be ethical and effective.

10

Which office item can make your influence stick?

If you're reading this at your desk, the answer to the question above may be within arm's reach. What could it be? Paper clips? Pens? Pencils? Pads? Protractor? Planners? Paperweights? Printer? Your office drawers are full of practical items. Which can make your influence stick?

Social scientist Randy Garner wondered whether sticky notes – the best known are Post-it notes, made by the 3M Corp. – might have the power to enhance compliance with a written request made to another person. In an intriguing study, he sent out surveys to people with a request to complete them. The survey was accompanied by either (a) a handwritten sticky note requesting completion of the survey, which was attached to a cover letter; (b) a similar handwritten message on the cover letter; or (c) the cover letter and survey alone.

That little yellow square packed quite a persuasive punch: more than 75 per cent of the people who received the survey with the sticky-note request filled it out and returned it, whereas only 48 per cent of the second group and 36 per cent of the third group did so. But what made it work? Could it be the simple fact that sticky notes are attention-grabbing in all their neon glory?

Garner asked himself the same question. To test this

possibility, he sent out a new batch of surveys. This time, a third of the surveys came with a Post-it note with a handwritten request, a third came with a blank Post-it note, and a third had no Post-it note at all. If the plus of using Post-its is simply that the neon-yellow colour draws people's peepers to the paper, then response rates should be equally high for both sets of Post-it note surveys. But that turns out not to be the case. The handwritten sticky note outperformed its competition, with a response rate of 69 per cent compared with 43 per cent for the surveys with a blank sticky note and 34 per cent for the surveys with no sticky note.

So what's the explanation? Although no one's going to break a sweat looking for a Post-it note, slapping it on a cover sheet and handwriting a message on it, Garner suggests that people do recognise the extra effort and personal touch that this requires, and they feel the need to reciprocate this personal touch by agreeing to the request. After all, reciprocity is the social glue that helps bring and keep people together in cooperative relationships – and you can bet that it's a stronger adhesive than the kind you find on the back of a sticky note.

In fact, the evidence is even more telling. Garner found that placing a personalised sticky note on the survey did more than simply persuade more people to respond to the survey: those who filled out the survey with the handwritten sticky-note message returned it more promptly and gave more detailed and attentive answers to the questions. And when the researcher made the note even more personal in nature by adding his initials and 'Thank you!' to the handwritten message, the response rate shot up even higher.

Broadly speaking, this research provides a valuable insight into human behaviour: that the more personalised you make a request, the more likely you'll be to get someone to agree to it.

More specifically, this research shows that in the office, in the community or even at home, a personalised sticky note could highlight the importance of your reports and communications and prevent them from becoming the proverbial needle in a haystack of other reports, letters and mailings that are vying for attention. What's more, the timeliness and quality of compliance with your request are likely to be enhanced as well.

What's the bottom line? If you use personalised messages for your persuasive practices, the 3M Corp. won't be the only ones who profit from it.

11

Why should restaurants ditch their baskets of mints?

Unless we're on our way to slay a vampire, when we've finished eating a garlicky meal at a restaurant many of us are happy to see that there is a basket of mints by the exit. Although this arrangement certainly leaves a good taste in your mouth, could it be that having the mints in this location might not exactly be the sweetest arrangement for the restaurant and its waiting staff?

Many restaurants provide the sweets in a different and far more effective way: the food server will provide them in the form of a little gift at the end of a meal. Even though the gift is nothing more than a chocolate or some other sweet presented on a silver platter along with your bill, these sweets can, in fact, be remarkably persuasive.

Behavioural scientist David Strohmetz and colleagues conducted an experiment to determine what effect, if any, giving a little confectionery to patrons at the end of the meal would have on food servers' tips. In one test condition, when presenting the bill the food servers included a single sweet for each diner. What happened to the average tip from those diners compared with a control group who received no sweet? The researchers found an increase in tips – not a huge one, but an increase all the same of 3.3 per cent. In the second condition, the servers gave two sweets to each diner. Despite the fact that this was only an additional penny-a-piece sweet, tips were 14.1 per cent higher than when no sweet was given. All of this is reasonably predictable, considering what we know about the norm of reciprocity – the more a person gives to us, the more we feel obligated to give in return. But what factors make a gift or favour most persuasive of all? The third condition in this study provides us with the answer.

For the third group of diners, the servers first gave one sweet to each person at the table. They then turned away from the table, signalling that they were leaving. Before exiting the area completely, however, they turned back towards the diners, reached into a pocket and placed a second sweet on the table for each diner. By making this gesture it was almost as if they were saying to their customers, 'Oh, for you nice people, here is an extra sweet each.' The result? A 23 per cent increase in tips.

This study suggests that there are three factors that help make a gift or favour more persuasive and as a result more likely to be reciprocated. The first factor is that what is given is seen by the recipient as significant. Giving diners two sweets compared with one had the effect of boosting the increase in their tips from 3.3 per cent to over 14 per cent. Notice that significant need not mean costly. Two sweets cost no more than a few pennies. But notice also an additional important element in the third condition. From an economic perspective, the second and third conditions are the same. In both conditions, the diners were given two sweets by their server at the end of the meal. There was no difference in the *amount* given, but there was a difference in the *way* the gift was given. It's this insight which provides us with two additional factors that make a gift more persuasive – the extent to which it is unexpected and the extent to which it is personalised. The diners in this third condition probably concluded that after they were given the one sweet and the waiter had turned away, this would be their final inter-action with him – and that's why the gift was unexpected. And, by making it seem as if he felt a special liking for that table's diners, the waiter made the gift of the second sweet appear to be personalised.

Of course, if servers used this tactic on every table, not only would they be seen as unethical by the patrons, but the tactic wouldn't work for long. As soon as diners noticed that the same practice was being used on everyone, the additional sweet would no longer be experienced as significant, personalised or unexpected. Instead, it would be viewed as a cunning trick that would backfire on the servers. It is possible, however, to use the lessons of the study in an ethical manner. To ensure that any gift that you give or favour that you perform is most appreci-ated, be sure to take some time to find out what, to the recipi-ent, would be genuinely personal, significant and unexpected.

Even if we consider only the findings from the first two con-ditions of the study, however, we can see that a restaurant that chooses to put its mints by the exit may be missing out on an important opportunity to have the food servers give a token of appreciation to their patrons, and receive a token of apprecia-tion in return. Even though the cost of these sweets may be only a few pennies, the servers can show each diner that he or she is worth far more to them.

12

What's the pull of having no strings attached?

Earlier we discussed how most hotels that have towel reuse programmes try to persuade their guests to join in by reminding
them about the importance of protecting the environment.
Some hotels, however, take an additional step towards creating
a cooperative atmosphere in their appeals: they offer guests an
incentive for their cooperation. In these incentive-based messages, the towel reuse card indicates that if the guests choose to
reuse their towels, the hotel will donate a percentage of the
energy savings to a non-profit environmental protection
organisation.

It's easy to see why the designers of these signs would think
that incentives would be effective. Most of us intuitively feel
that incentives work: ice-cream cones excel at persuading kids to
clean their rooms, carefully timed treats can help even old dogs
learn new tricks, and pay cheques have the power to limit the
number of times we hit the snooze button before we get out of
bed and go to work. Although the incentives being offered would
not directly benefit the guests, it still seems likely that guests
would be motivated to participate in the programme because of
the additional benefit to the environment being offered. But
does it work?

To find out, two of us conducted another study at the same

hotel. This time, some rooms displayed towel reuse cards that featured the standard environmental appeal, whereas other rooms displayed ones using this incentive-based cooperation approach. When we examined the data, we found that this new appeal produced no improvement over the standard environmental protection sign. Why?

Despite the factors that could support this type of approach, there is actually good reason to believe that a small shift needs to occur in that message to make it more persuasive than the standard approach. After all, there's little social obligation to cooperate with someone who offers you something only on the condition that you make the first move. That kind of exchange is simply an economic transaction. On the other hand, there's a hugely powerful sense of obligation embodied in the norm of reciprocation to return favours already received. Little wonder, then, that the incentive-based cooperation appeal was no more effective in persuading the guests to reuse their towels than the standard appeal – it contained no social obligation to comply with the request, as the hotel gave nothing first.

This suggests that the hotels using the incentive-based cards may have got the idea of cooperation right but the sequence wrong. Considering our knowledge of how the norm of reciprocity operates, perhaps a more effective way to increase participation in the programme would be to reverse the sequence of favour-doing – in other words, for the hotel to *give the donation first* with no strings attached, and *then* ask guests to join in by reusing their towels. This idea formed the basis for a third message that we included in the study.

This third message was similar to the incentive-based message in that it discussed a donation to a non-profit environmental protection organisation. Rather than offering to make the donation only on the condition that the guests took the first step in the cooperative effort, however, this appeal stated that the hotel *had already donated* to such an organisation – and that it did so *on behalf of its guests*. It then asked the guests to reciprocate this gesture by reusing their towels during their stay.

Impressively, the reciprocation-based message yielded a towel reuse rate that was 45 per cent higher than the incentive-based message. This finding is particularly interesting in light of the fact that these appeals have nearly the same content but convey quite different messages. Although both these messages informed the guests that the hotel was donating money to a non-profit environmental protection agency, the reciprocation-based message informed the guests that the hotel had initiated the joint effort, using the forces of reciprocation and social obligation to prompt guests to participate.

Along with data from other research studies, these findings make it clear that when we're trying to solicit cooperation from other people – be they co-workers, clients, students or acquaint-ances – we should offer them help in a way that's genuinely and completely unconditional. Approaching the potentially coop-erative relationship in this way should not only increase the chance that you'll gain their consent in the first place, but also ensure that the cooperation you do receive is built on a solid foundation of trust and mutual appreciation, rather than on a much weaker incentive system. You'll also find this approach to be much longer-lasting. Otherwise, the moment the incentive you've been promising or awarding can no longer be offered or is no longer desired by the other person, the brittle foundation of the relationship may crack, and the bridge you've built up may come crashing down.

13

Do favours behave like bread or like wine?

In several of the previous chapters, we have offered evidence that by first providing a gift, service or favour for someone we create a social obligation in the recipient to reciprocate. Whether that gift concerns providing some useful information, helping out a colleague with a favour, placing a personalised sticky note on a request we make to others or, in the case of Bobby Fischer, putting a whole country on the map, there is a social obligation to do as we've been done by. But what happens to the influence of those gifts and favours as time passes? Are favours like bread, growing stale in the mind of the recipient, losing value over time? Or are they more like wine, getting better and increasing in value with age? According to researcher Francis Flynn, the answer to this question depends on whether you do the favour or receive it.

Flynn conducted a survey of employees working in the customer service department of a large US airline. This particular business context is one in which co-workers commonly exchange favours by helping one another to cover shifts. The researcher asked half of the employees to consider a time when they had performed a favour for a co-worker, while the other half were asked to consider a time when they had received a favour. All the employees in the study were then asked to indicate the perceived value of the favour and also to specify how long ago the favour was performed. The results of the survey revealed that recipients of the favour perceived it as more valuable immediately after it was performed but less valuable as time passed. Favour-doers, on the other hand, showed just the opposite effect: they placed a lower value on the favour immediately after it was performed but then placed greater value on it as time went by.

One possibility is that, as time goes by, the memory of the event gets distorted; and since people have the tendency to see themselves in the best possible light, receivers may think they didn't need all that much help at the time, while doers may think they went the extra mile.

These findings have implications for our effectiveness in persuading others both inside and outside the workplace. If you've done a favour for a colleague or an acquaintance, that favour will likely have the most impact on that person's desire to reciprocate within a short period of time following the favour. If you're the recipient of a favour, however, you need to be aware of the tendency of people in your position to downplay that favour as time goes by. If you fail to recognise the full value of the favour weeks, months or even years after it has occurred, this may ultimately damage your relationship with the favour-doer. If you are the doer of the favour, you may tend to think ill of the recipient owing to his or her reticence to pay back what you have given. So what can be done to maximise the value of the favours we provide if this value might diminish in the eyes of the receiver over time? One way might be to recognise the value of the gift or favour you have provided at the time by telling the receiver that you were happy to help because you know 'that if the situation was ever reversed, I'm sure that you would do the same for me'.

A second and potentially more risky strategy might be to restate the value of the previous gift before making a subsequent request in the future. Of course, you should consider carefully the words you choose when taking this approach. Saying something like 'Remember when I helped you out a few weeks ago? Well, now its payback time, pal!' is destined to fail. But a gentle reminder, such as 'How useful did you find the report I sent to you?', might be a good thing to say before you make your request.

Although there's no universal method of influencing others 100 per cent of the time, we're certain that understanding all the factors that influence favour valuation is a good start. And if all else fails, just remember one simple rule of favour exchange: just as you'll catch more flies with honey than with vinegar, you'll definitely earn more favours with a bottle of vintage wine than with last week's loaf of bread.

14

How can a foot in the door lead to great strides?

Imagine that your house is situated in a wealthy, picturesque community – the kind of neighbourhood where people take great pride in their immaculate hedges, their perfect lawns and their freshly painted white picket fences. It's an area where estate agents never have a problem selling houses. In fact they will most likely have a waiting list of people wanting to move into the area. Imagine further that one day someone from the local Road Traffic Safety Committee knocks on your door and asks whether you'd be willing to support the Drive Carefully Through Our Neighbourhood campaign by placing a large sign measuring 6 feet by 3 feet and stating 'DRIVE CAREFULLY' on your front lawn. His assurance that workmen, and not you, will be employed to dig the holes in which the billboard posts will be placed does little to ease your concerns.

How many people do you think would agree to such a request? According to an experiment conducted by social psychologists Jonathan Freedman and Scott Fraser, 17 per cent of homeowners in a posh neighbourhood like the one described above agreed to this request. But astonishingly, the researchers were able to obtain a 76 per cent compliance rate from a different set of residents simply by making one seemingly insignificant addition to their request. What was the addition, and what does it tell us about how to persuade others effectively?

A different research assistant approached this separate group of residents two weeks before this burdensome request and asked them whether they'd be willing to display a very small, relatively inconspicuous sign in their window that read 'BE A SAFE DRIVER'. Because it was such a small request, almost all these residents agreed. Two weeks later, when someone else came to their home and asked them whether they'd be willing to place that unsightly billboard on their otherwise perfectly manicured lawn, they were much more inclined to agree.

But why would such a simple additional request, a strategy that the researchers refer to as the 'foot-in-the-door technique', result in this astonishing boost in compliance with the much larger request? The evidence suggests that after agreeing to the request, the residents came to see themselves as committed to worthy causes such as safe driving. When these homeowners were approached a couple of weeks later, they were motivated to act consistently with this perception of themselves as concerned citizens.

There are countless uses of the foot-in-the-door technique, including in sales. For example, one astute sales expert advises, 'The general idea is to pave the way for full-line distribution by starting with a small order ... Look at it this way – when a person has signed an order for your merchandise, even though the profit is so small it hardly compensates for the time and effort of making the call, [he or she] is no longer a prospect – [he or she] is a customer.'

In cases in which a business can't secure even a small initial product purchase, this commitment- and consistency-based strategy can be applied in other ways. For example, potential clients who are reluctant to use your service may be more inclined to do so if they're first asked to take a small step, such as agreeing to an initial ten-minute appointment.

Similarly, a marketing research department is more likely to get people to answer a large number of survey questions by first asking them whether they'd be willing to answer a brief survey. In fact, Freedman and Fraser conducted another experiment whose results support this last point. In that experiment, a research assistant called up homeowners and asked them if they'd be willing to participate in a survey. Specifically, they said the following:

The survey will involve five or six men from our staff coming into your home some morning for about two hours to enumerate and classify all the household products that you have. They will have to have full freedom in your house to go through the cupboards and storage places. Then all this information will be used in the writing of the reports for our public service publication, 'The Guide'.

In response to this very inconvenient request, 22 per cent of the homeowners agreed – pretty amazing, considering that these kinds of intrusive behaviours usually require a search warrant!

The researchers called a second set of residents three days prior to this invasive request. In this earlier call, homeowners were asked the following, to which the great majority agreed:

We are calling you this morning to ask if you would answer a number of questions about what household products you use so that we could have this information for our public service publication, 'The Guide'. Would you be willing to give us this information for our survey?

What happened three days later? Nearly 53 per cent of these homeowners agreed to the large request.

Such an approach can also be applied to two of the most resistant targets that you're ever likely to come across – your children and yourself. Resistant children who easily find excuses not to do their homework or tidy their room are more likely to be persuaded if they're first asked to take a small step in that direction. This could take the form of asking them to spend a short period of time with you working on their homework or requesting that they put a cherished toy back in its box when they've finished playing with it. As long as they feel they've said yes to the first small request voluntarily – rather than through coercion – the psychological momentum should propel them towards scholastic success and cleaner living quarters.

In the case of influencing ourselves, rather than setting a large and seemingly insurmountable target to improve, say, our fitness levels, we would be well advised to set a task for ourselves that is small enough that we would have no excuses for not completing it at least once – for example, taking a short walk around the block. As a result, we should find ourselves gradually increasing our degree of commitment to meet the larger fitness goals. Confucius said, 'A journey of a thousand miles begins with a single step.' There may be no better way to get us off the sofa and starting to make great strides.

15

How can you become a Jedi master of social influence?

A long time ago (about a quarter of a century ago, to be exact), in a galaxy far, far away, Luke Skywalker gained the ultimate form of compliance: he persuaded Darth Vader to turn against the evil emperor, saving his own life and restoring hope and peace to the galaxy. What social influence principle did he use to secure this compliance, and how can that principle be used to help your attempts to be a major Force in your industry?

The movie *Return of the Jedi*, the final episode of the Star Wars series, includes a scene in which Luke Skywalker turns to Darth Vader and says, 'I know there's still good in you. There's good in you, I can sense it.' Is it possible that these simple words could have persuaded Vader – or at the very least planted the seeds of persuasion – to come over to the Light Side? If we look at social psychological research, the answer appears to be yes.

The strategy demonstrated in these words, known as the labelling technique, involves assigning a trait, attitude, belief or other label to a person and then making a request of that person that's consistent with that label. In an effective demonstration of this strategy, researchers Alice Tybout and Richard Yalch showed how the labelling technique could be used to increase the likelihood that people would vote on an election day. They interviewed a large number of potential voters, and randomly told half of them that, based on their responses, they could be characterised as 'above-average citizens likely to vote and participate in political events'. The other half of the interviewees were informed that they could be characterised as about average in terms of these interests, beliefs and behaviours. Those respondents labelled as being good citizens and having a high likelihood of voting not only came to see themselves as better citizens than those labelled as average, but were also 15 per cent more likely to vote in an election held one week later.

Of course, the labelling technique isn't limited to political domains such as choosing our next leader or, in Luke Skywalker's case, deposing the emperor. There are a number of ways in which you can use this technique in your business dealings and other interactions. For example, let's say that someone in your work team is struggling with a particular project you have asked him to manage. Perhaps this team member is losing confidence in his abilities to provide what the project requires. A useful approach, assuming that you still believe him to be capable of the task, would be to remind him how hard-working and persevering he is. You should even point out examples of previous times when he has triumphed over similar challenges and successfully delivered. Teachers, trainers and parents can apply this labelling strategy to sculpt desired behaviours by pointing out to their audience that they regard them as just the type of person who would thrive when given this sort of challenge. This strategy works for adults and children alike. For instance, research that one of us conducted with several colleagues showed that when teachers tell children that they seem like students who care about having good handwriting, the kids spent more of their free time practising their handwriting – even when they thought no one was around to watch.

A company's relationship with its clients can also be

strengthened in this way. You might be familiar with the way many airlines have taken advantage of this principle: when the chief flight attendant tells passengers at the end of the flight, 'We know you have many airlines to choose from, so we thank you for choosing ours,' he or she is using a derivative of the labelling technique, reminding you implicitly that if there are so many choices out there, you must have chosen this airline for a reason. Assigned the label of having confidence in that airline, passengers should come to see themselves as having even greater confidence in their choice (and in the airline). Similarly, you can use the technique to remind clients that their decision to deal with your company shows their confidence in your company and in you, and that you appreciate and will make good on that confidence.

Just remember, as tempting as it might be to move over to the Dark Side with this strategy, like all other influence strategies it should be used only ethically – in other words, only when the trait, attitude, belief or other label accurately reflects the audience's natural capabilities, experiences or personality. Of course, we know you wouldn't even think of using this strategy in an unethical manner. After all, we sense much good in you.

16

How can a simple question drastically increase support for you and your ideas?

As any politician will tell you, in election periods candidates are under enormous pressure to find ways not only to convince the electorate of their qualities, but also to draw those supporters to the polls on election day. Whereas, in the United States at least, some campaigners will pour more and more money into television advertisements, mailings and media appearances, the truly astute candidate – and probably the winner – will look to harness not just the art of persuasion, but the science of persuasion as well.

A stark example from the 2000 US presidential election, where only 537 votes made a huge difference, ensures that we are more aware than ever that every single vote counts. During that infamous election, with the media and the USA as a whole focused on myriad controversies, even the tiniest boost in voter turnout in one direction or the other could have had a large impact on the outcome. What simple strategy could have been used to draw supporters from either side to the polls?

The answer involves merely asking potential voters to predict whether they will vote on election day and to provide a reason for their prediction. When social scientist Anthony Greenwald and his colleagues tried this technique on potential voters on the eve of one such election day, those who were asked to make a prediction yielded a turnout rate that was 25 per cent higher than those who weren't asked (86.7 per cent compared with 61.5 per cent).

There are two important psychological steps involved in this technique. First, when people are asked to predict whether they'll engage in a socially desirable behaviour in the future, they're going to feel compelled to say yes because that's what wins social approval under the circumstances. Considering the importance that society places on voting, it'd be mighty difficult for the respondents to back out by saying they were planning to stay at home to watch a TV programme on civic responsibility instead. It's no surprise, then, that in this study 100 per cent of all the survey respondents asked to make a prediction about their voting behaviour claimed that they would indeed vote.

Second, after most (if not all) of these people have publicly stated that they'll perform the socially desirable behaviour, they'll be motivated to behave consistently with the commitment they have just made. As another example, one restaurant owner greatly reduced the percentage of no-shows (people who booked a table but didn't honour the reservation and didn't call to cancel it) by having his receptionist change what she said when taking a reservation from 'Please call if you have to cancel' to 'Will you please call if you have to cancel?' Of course, nearly all customers committed themselves to calling by saying 'yes' to that question. More importantly, they then felt the need to abide by their commitment: the no-show rate dropped from 30 per cent to 10 per cent.

Consequently, an easy method for candidates to get more of their supporters to the polls is to have volunteers call these self-proclaimed supporters, ask them whether they'll vote in the next election and wait for the 'yes'. If the caller then adds: 'We'll mark you down as a "yes" and I'll let the others know as well,' the commitment has three components that potentially cement that person's commitment: the commitment becomes voluntary, active and publicly declared to others.

What lessons can we draw that can be employed effectively in the workplace and in the broader community? Let's say that you're thinking about doing a charity run for your favourite non-profit organisation, but you don't want to sign up unless you are fairly certain you'll get a lot of donations. Asking family, friends and co-workers whether they think they'll donate will not only give you an idea of their initial support for your undertaking, but will also increase the likelihood that they *will* donate should you decide to join the run.

As another example of this strategy, imagine that you manage a team of people and you recognise that the success of a new initiative doesn't just depend on gaining verbal support from others in your team, but also on turning that support into meaningful action. Rather than just explaining to team members what benefits they would derive from supporting a particular initiative, you should ask them whether they would be willing to support such an initiative and wait for a 'yes' in response. Following that agreement, you should ask them to describe their reasons for supporting the initiative.

Whatever your role, be it as manager, teacher, salesperson, politician or fund-raiser, we think you'll find that if you use this strategy, you'll probably elicit another important vote – a strong vote of confidence in your work.

17

What is the active ingredient in lasting commitments?

The Amway Corporation, one of America's most profitable direct-selling companies, encourages its sales personnel to soar to greater heights by providing the following advice:

One final tip before you get started: Set a goal and write it down. Whatever the goal, the important thing is that you set it, so you've got something for which to aim – and that you write it down. There is something magical about writing things down. So set a goal and write it down. When you reach that goal, set another and write that down. You'll be off and running.

Why might writing down our goals be so effective in strengthening our commitments, even when the content of what we write down stays private?

Put simply, commitments that are made actively have more staying power than those that are made passively. In a recent demonstration of both the power and the subtlety of active commitments, social scientists Delia Cioffi and Randy Garner solicited college student volunteers for an AIDS education project to be carried out at local schools. The researchers set up the study so that the students were given one of two different sets of instructions. Those who received the active instructions were told that if they wanted to volunteer, they should indicate this by filling out a form stating that they were willing to participate. In contrast, those who received the passive instructions were told that if they wanted to volunteer, they should leave blank the form stating that they were not willing to participate.

The researchers found that the percentage of people who agreed to volunteer didn't differ as a function of whether the instructions invited active or passive responding. Yet there was quite an astonishing difference in the percentage of people who actually showed up to take part several days later. Of those whose agreement was passive, only 17 per cent appeared as promised. What about those who agreed to participate through active means? Of those, 49 per cent kept their promises. In all, the clear majority of those who appeared as scheduled (74 per cent) were those who had actively agreed to volunteer for the programme.

Why are commitments that are written (and therefore active) so much more successful at eliciting participation? People make judgements about themselves based on observations of their own behaviours, and they infer more about themselves based on their actions than on their non-actions. In support of this explanation, Cioffi and Garner found that those who volunteered actively were more likely to attribute their decisions to their own personality traits, preferences and ideals than were those who volunteered passively.

What can active commitments do for your influence attempts? Let's say that it is the time of year when many of us traditionally make a very specific commitment – the New Year resolution. Writing down and describing in detail the resolution you have committed to, rather than just thinking about it, and also describing what steps you will take to achieve your chosen goal, could be helpful to you, especially if you then go on to show your friends and family those written commitments.

If you're a sales manager, asking members of your sales team to write down their goals will help strengthen their commitment to those goals and ultimately boost everyone's bottom line. Similarly, it is wise to ensure that, during a meeting, participants write down and publicly share the actions that they have agreed to take.

An example in the retail environment provides a further illustration of the power of writing things down. Many stores offer their customers the opportunity to spread the cost of purchasing products over a number of months or even years by signing up for a store credit card or some other finance product. Retailers find that customers are less likely to cancel the agreement if they, rather than the salesperson, fill out the application form. These data show that to maximise commitments to the initiatives you undertake jointly with clients and business associates, you should arrange for all parties involved to take an active role in filling out any relevant business agreements.

Active commitments have the potential to be used to great effect throughout the healthcare industry. In recent years, healthcare providers have reported that more patients than ever have been failing to show up to their appointments at the scheduled time. In fact, a National Health Service survey indicates that 7 million medical appointments were missed by patients in one year alone, a staggering figure that has important financial and medical consequences. In what way might active commitments help alleviate the problem? When we make appointments for our next visit – whether it's for a routine check-up or important surgery – it's standard practice for the receptionist or administrator of the unit to write down the date and time of that next appointment on a little reminder card. With such a routine, however, the patient's role is passive rather than active. Instead, asking patients to fill out the card themselves should prove to be an effective and low-cost strategy to reduce the no-show rates.

Finally, as with many other approaches described in this book, active commitments can be useful to generate compliance in our personal lives, too. A small but psychologically significant action such as securing an active, written commitment from our children, neighbours, friends, partners or even ourselves can often mean the difference between being able to influence others effectively and soliciting commitments that others have all the intention in the world of fulfilling but somehow never get around to.

18

How can you fight consistency with consistency?

According to Oscar Wilde, 'Consistency is the last refuge of the unimaginative.' A similarly disdainful Ralph Waldo Emerson said, 'A foolish consistency is the hobgoblin of little minds.' And finally, Aldous Huxley noted, 'The only truly consistent people are dead.' Why is it more likely that these famous authors made these statements when they were young whippersnappers than when they were elderly sages, and what could this mean for your influence attempts?

These authors' opinions notwithstanding, as we discussed earlier in the book, people generally prefer their behaviours to be consistent with their pre-existing attitudes, statements, values and actions. But how does the ageing process alter this inclination? Along with lead researcher Stephanie Brown and another colleague, one of us conducted a study showing that people's preference for consistency grows stronger as they get older. This is likely to be the case because inconsistency can be emotionally upsetting, and older people have a greater motivation to avoid emotionally upsetting experiences.

This finding has important implications for how we try to influence older people. For example, suppose you work for a company that's attempting to market a range of new products to a more mature audience. This research suggests that this particular demographic is going to be more resistant to change than others, as change might make older people feel that their actions have become inconsistent with their previously made commitments. In such a case, you'd be well advised to focus your messages on how purchasing and using the product are consistent with the audience's pre-existing values, beliefs and practices. The same lesson can be applied in other domains, such as convincing an old-timer in a work team to switch to a new system, or even getting one's elderly parents to take their medication.

But do people really give up their previous behaviours that easily – simply by being informed that the new behaviours we're suggesting are consistent with their previously held values, beliefs and practices? From their point of view, remaining consistent with those decisions is probably a good thing. And we all know how frustrating it can be to deal with people who are routinely inconsistent, who constantly change their mind, who are easily influenced by the very next message they hear.

Dealing with people like this requires us to do something else in addition to simply pointing out how our proposal aligns with what they have previously declared to be important to them. To ensure that our message is optimally persuasive, we need not only to free them from their previous commitment, but also avoid framing their previous decision as a mistake. Perhaps the most productive way would be to praise the previous decision and describe it as correct '*at the time they made it*'. Pointing out that the previous choices they made were the right ones '*given the evidence and information they had at the time*' can help free them from their commitment and allow them to focus on your proposal without the need for loss of face or inconsistency.

Now, after such a 'pre-persuasion' statement, your next

message, still aligned to their overall values, beliefs and practices, has legs. In the same way that a painter will prepare a canvas before painting, a medical professional will prepare surgical equipment before operating and a sports coach will prepare her team before a match, a persuasive appeal requires preparation, too. And sometimes such preparation requires us not only to consider how to pitch our message but also to pay attention to previous messages and reactions. As the saying goes, the best way to ride a horse is *in the direction that the horse is going.* Only by first aligning yourself with the direction of the horse is it possible to then slowly and deliberately steer it where you'd like to go. Simply trying to pull the horse in the desired direction immediately will just wear you out – and you'll probably just upset the horse in the process.

19

What persuasion tip can you borrow from Benjamin Franklin?

Born in 1706, Benjamin Franklin is renowned for being a leading author, politician, diplomat, scientist, publisher, philosopher and inventor. As a politician, perhaps more than any other, he invented the idea of an American nation. As a diplomat during the American Revolution, he secured the French alliance that helped to make independence possible. As a scientist, he was a major figure for his discoveries and theories regarding electricity. And as an inventor, he was responsible for the creation of bifocals, the odometer and the lightning rod. But it's what he discovered about how to win the respect of his opposition – by inconveniencing them, no less – that may be the most electrifying discovery of all.

When Franklin was in the Pennsylvania legislature, he was deeply bothered by the staunch political opposition and hostility of another legislator. Franklin himself best explains how he set out to win this man's respect and even his friendship:

I did not, however, aim at gaining his favour by paying any servile respect to him, but, after some time, took this other method. Having heard that he had in his library a certain very scarce and curious book, I wrote a note to him, expressing my desire of perusing that book, and requesting he would do me the favour of lending it to me for a few days. He sent it immediately, and I return'd it in about a week with another note, expressing strongly my sense of the favour. When we next met in the House, he spoke to me (which he had never done before), and with great civility; and he ever after manifested a readiness to serve me on all occasions, so that we became great friends, and our friendship continued to his death. This is another instance of the truth of an old maxim I had learned, which says, 'He that has once done you a kindness will be more ready to do you another, than he whom you yourself have obliged.'

Many years later, behavioural researchers Jon Jecker and David Landy set out to see whether Franklin was right. In one study, participants won some money from the experimenter in a contest. Afterwards, one group of participants was approached by the experimenter, who asked them whether they'd be willing to give back the money because he was using his own funds and had little left. (Almost all agreed.) Another group of participants was not approached with any request. All the participants were then anonymously surveyed about how much they liked the experimenter.

Was Franklin's strategy, as illogical as it sounds, supported by this experiment? Indeed it was. Jecker and Landy found that those who were asked to do the favour rated the experimenter more favourably than did those who were not asked to give back the money.

Why? We know from other studies that people are strongly motivated to change their attitudes in ways that are consistent with their behaviours. When Franklin's opponent found himself doing a favour for someone he didn't care for, he probably had to say to himself, 'Why am I going out of my way to help out this person I don't even like? Perhaps Franklin's not so bad after all. Come to think of it, maybe he does have some redeeming qualities …'

Franklin's strategy lends itself to managing relationships in any number of different environments. To take one, we often need assistance from a co-worker, neighbour or colleague who, for one reason or another, doesn't view us in a particularly favourable light. We might be reluctant to ask for the favour because we're afraid this person will like us even less. Rather than ask, a more typical tendency is to put off the request, potentially delaying a timely accomplishment of the task at hand. The results of this research indicate that such hesitation is unwarranted.

Now, in the case of some objectionable people, asking for a favour might seem to be a rather brave thing to do. But consider the following: if you currently have nothing to show from your communications (or non-communications) with this person, the worst thing that will happen is that you'll end up with the same nothing. Try it. You'll truly have nothing to lose.

20

When can asking for a little go a long way?

Presumably it was someone very little who first said, 'Good things come in small packages.' Whoever coined the phrase, it's clear that this person understood the power of thinking big by going small.

Throughout this book, we've attempted to provide evidence to support our claims that we can successfully and ethically move people to say yes. But in certain situations and environments, it's also important to understand why people say no to reasonable requests, such as a request to donate to a legitimate charity.

Along with several colleagues, one of us set out to do just that. We thought that when asked to make a donation, even those who would like to support the charity in some way say no because they can't afford to donate very much and they assume that the small amount they can afford wouldn't do much to help the cause. Based on this reasoning, we thought that one way to urge people to donate in such a situation would be to inform them that even an extremely small sum would be helpful, essentially legitimising small contributions.

To test this hypothesis, our research assistants went door to door to request donations for the American Cancer Society. After introducing themselves, they asked the residents, 'Would you be willing to help by giving a donation?' For half the residents, the request ended there. For the other half, however, the research assistant added, 'Even a penny will help.'

When we analysed the results, we found that this diminutive disc of copper and zinc was worth its weight in persuasive gold. Consistent with our hypothesis, people in the 'even a penny will help' half of the sample were almost twice as likely as those in the other half to donate to the cause (50 per cent versus 28.6 per cent).

On the face of it, the study suggests that when you want assistance from others, simply pointing out that even a small offering on their part would be acceptable and worthwhile to you is likely to be an effective strategy. Still, is there a possibility that adopting a strategy of 'even a penny will help' could backfire? Even though almost double the number of people donated when told that even a penny would help, might they have donated a smaller amount, less than they ordinarily would, than those in the other half of the sample? To check on this potential drawback, we looked at the size of donation amounts and were happy to find that there was no difference in the average donation per contributor. What this means is that the 'even a penny will help' request should come out ahead of a standard request not only in terms of the number of people who donate, but also in the overall amount raised by each request. In our study, for instance, for every hundred people we asked, we collected $72 in donations from the first half of the sample compared with only $44 from the other half.

There are several applications of the 'even a penny will help' approach in the workplace. To co-workers regarding a community project, 'Just an hour of your time would really help.' To a colleague whose handwriting is illegible, 'Just a little more clarity would help.' To a busy prospective client whose needs must be more fully understood, 'Even a brief initial phone call would help.' The chances are that this little step in the right direction won't prove so little after all.

21

Start low or start high? Which will make people buy?

What can items such as gum chewed by Britney Spears, a Papa Smurf commemorative plate or a broken laser pointer teach us about how to most effectively sell goods and services through a competitive bidding process? An examination of how people list their 'treasures' on eBay can in fact be very revealing.

eBay Inc. is the company that manages ebay.com, the online auction and shopping website where people and businesses buy and sell goods and services worldwide. It was founded in 1995 in San Jose, California, by a computer programmer named Pierre Omidyar, who ran a consulting company called the Echo Bay Technology Group. When he went to register his consultancy group's website, he found that echobay.com had already been taken by the gold mining company Echo Bay Mines, so he shortened the company name and ebay.com was born. The very first item to appear on eBay was Omidyar's broken laser pointer, which he sold for $14.83. Astonished that someone would want to buy such an item, he contacted the winning bidder and asked whether he understood that the laser pointer was broken. Responding to the e-mail, the buyer explained: 'I'm a collector of broken laser pointers.'

In 2006, eBay registered some $6 billion in sales on a site where it is now possible to buy pretty much anything you can imagine – and sometimes items beyond the realm of imagination. In recent years, the original Hollywood sign and one of the Channel Tunnel boring machines were both auctioned on eBay. An Arizona man successfully managed to sell his prized air guitar for $5.50 even though he pointed out that bidders were in fact buying nothing, and in 2005 the clearly outraged wife of a UK radio disc jockey sold his beloved Lotus Esprit sports car for a 'Buy It Now' price of 50 pence after she heard him flirting on the airwaves with a glamour model. The car sold in five minutes.

Clearly ebay.com has identified a hugely successful business model, the basis of which is online auctioneering. In fact, many companies have adopted similar models using online bidding processes and systems to secure tenders and choose vendors. Because of the inherent similarities between an online auction's bidding processes and a business's competitive bidding process, observing how sellers most effectively sell their stuff on websites like eBay can teach us quite a bit about how to most effectively manage a company's competitive bidding process.

Behavioural scientist Gillian Ku and her colleagues suggested that when the initial price for an item is high, as a potential buyer you're likely to think it's worth more than if the initial price were lower. They seriously questioned, however, whether the increase in perceived value that comes with a high starting price would actually lead to a higher final sale price. Instead, they suggested that lower starting prices would lead to a higher final sale price for three reasons.

First, because the starting prices for auctions act as something of a barrier to entry, lower starting prices are better for encouraging participation by as many people as possible in the bidding for an item. Second, the increase in traffic – reflected in the total number of bids as well as the number of different bidders – afforded by these lower initial prices acts as social proof for new potential bidders. In other words, prospective bidders considering an item that started off at a low price would find social validation that the item is of value because so many more people are also bidding on the item, and this validation would spur them to join the bidding. Third, bidders for items with low starting prices, especially those who get in early, are likely to spend more time and effort updating their bids; in an effort to justify the time and energy they've already spent on the bidding process, these bidders are more likely to stay committed to winning the auction by continuing to bid and raising their bids even higher.

These research findings suggest that if you are in the business of offering goods or services through any kind of competitive bidding process, starting the bidding at a fairly low price can be a way of enhancing the final sale price. There is, however, one very important caveat to consider: the researchers found that the social proof component was a critical factor in the enhanced effectiveness of the lower starting price. So, when the traffic for a particular item was constrained (for example, owing to a misspelling of the product name on eBay, which limits the number of prospective bidders who are likely to find the item through a typical search), the lower starting price was less effective. The implication is that the lower starting price is likely to be most effective when there's a possibility that many bidders would want your products but is likely to be least effective when the bidding is limited to only two parties.

Although putting this into practice might not earn you millions of extra dollars for your company's widgets or your family's antique thimble collection, at the very least it should help you earn enough to bid on that air guitar, should it come up for sale again.

22

How can you show off without being labelled a show-off?

If you're like most people, when you know best you want to tell the whole world about it. But even when you have the credentials to present yourself as an authority on a topic, there's a dilemma to overcome: in trying to convey your expertise to others, and in attempting to win them round, you might come across as boastful and conceited. As a result, others may like you less, and possibly even be less inclined to follow your advice. With unabashed self-promotion out of the question, what's a genuine expert to do?

One option is to get someone else to speak on your behalf. This approach has been widely accepted by speakers, authors, performers and other public communicators for many years. Arranging for someone else to describe your expertise and credentials to the audience will do wonders to convince them that they should listen to what you have to say, while also avoiding the damage that blatant self-promotion can cause. Ideally, this person would be a true believer in your skills and knowledge, and would volunteer to tell everyone how smart you are in the hope that you'll make the world a better place. Failing that, he'd be a paid representative.

But won't people be put off by the fact that the presenter is being paid to sing your praises? Not if they commit one of the most common errors that people make, which social psychologists often call the fundamental attribution error: when observing someone else's behaviour, we tend not to give sufficient weight to the role that situational factors (e.g. money) play in shaping that person's behaviour.

In a set of studies one of us conducted with lead researcher Jeffrey Pfeffer and two other colleagues, we argued that people do not take this information into account nearly as much as they should, which means that paying an intermediary to endorse your abilities should still be an effective form of persuasion. In one of those studies, participants were asked to imagine themselves in the role of senior editor for a book publisher, facing the task of dealing with an experienced and successful author. They were asked to read excerpts from a negotiation for a sizeable book advance. One group read excerpts touting the author's accomplishments spoken by the author's agent, whereas a second group read identical comments made by the author himself. The data verified our hypothesis: participants rated the author more favourably on nearly every scale – especially likeability – when the author's agent sang his praises as compared to when the author tooted his own horn.

This research confirms that having a skilled third party who will speak on your behalf can be a very productive and worthwhile strategy for conveying your expertise. (In fact, where possible, that third party should also negotiate on your behalf in terms of contract conditions and remuneration.) We'd also recommend that when giving a presentation to people who don't know you very well, you should arrange for someone else to introduce you to your audience. One of the most efficient ways of doing this is to have prepared a short biography of yourself. This needn't be lengthy, but it should at the very least contain some information about your background, training or education which makes it clear that you are qualified to speak on a certain topic. You could also include examples of successes that you've had in the area on which you'll be speaking.

Recently one of us had the opportunity to work with an estate agency that used this approach to an immediate and highly successful effect. The agency concerned has both a sales and a letting division. This meant that customers who called the office would typically first speak to a receptionist who, having identified which department they needed, would say, 'Oh, lettings, you need to speak to Sandra', or 'You need the sales department – let me put you through to Peter.'

In response to our recommendation that she should introduce her colleagues along with their credentials, the receptionist now not only tells enquiring customers which of her colleagues they should speak to but also something about her colleagues' expertise. Customers who want further information about lettings are now told, 'Oh, lettings, you need to speak to Sandra, who has over fifteen years' experience letting properties in this neighbourhood. Let me put you through now.' Similarly, customers who want more information about selling their property are now told, 'I'm going to put you through to Peter, our head of sales. Peter has twenty years' experience selling properties; in fact he recently sold a property very similar to yours.'

There are four notable features of this change. First, everything the receptionist tells her customers about her co-workers' experience is true. Sandra does have fifteen years' experience, and Peter is one of the most successful agency salespeople. But for Peter or Sandra to tell the customers this themselves would be seen as boastful and self-promoting, and as a result not nearly as persuasive. Second, it doesn't seem to matter that the introduction comes from someone who is clearly connected to Sandra and Peter, who will both obviously benefit from such an introduction. The third notable feature is how effective it is. Sandra, Peter and their colleagues report a significant rise in the number of appointments they are generating compared with when they hadn't been introduced. Point number four: the intervention cost next to nothing. Everyone knew of the wide-ranging expertise and experience that resided in the office. Everyone, that is, except the most important people of all – the company's potential customers.

But what if it's impractical to have someone else sing your praises? Is there another subtle way of demonstrating your competence without shouting it out? Indeed there is. To take an example, one of us was approached by a group of physician's assistants who were frustrated by their patients' non-compliance with important exercises that they needed to do to get healthier. No matter how hard they tried to convey the urgency of these exercises, patients would rarely follow their advice. When we asked to see the examining room, one thing immediately struck us: there were no credentials whatsoever on the wall – or anywhere else for that matter. After we had advised them to put their credentials in places where their patients could see them, the assistants reported a huge improvement in compliance. The lesson? Display your diplomas, certificates and awards to those you want to persuade. You've earned those credentials, and they, in turn, will help you earn your audience's trust.

23

What's the hidden danger of being the brightest person in the room?

Over drinks, pub patrons have been known to tell some dubious stories. 'I dated that supermodel before she got famous.' Sure you did. 'I could've won the fight, but I didn't want to hurt the other guy.' Uh-huh. Or 'I would have played football for England, but a bunion put an end to my career.' Right!

But on a cold and unpleasant February evening in 1953, two gentlemen walked into the Eagle public house in Cambridge, and after ordering their drinks, one of them announced to the other patrons what must have seemed like the tallest tale of all: 'We have found the secret of life.'

Although their claim might seem boastful and arrogant, it happened to be true. That morning, scientists James Watson and Francis Crick had indeed found the secret of life: they had discovered the double-helix structure of DNA, the biological material that carries life's genetic information.

On the fiftieth anniversary of what could be described as perhaps the most important scientific discovery of our time, Watson took part in an interview on the topic of this accomplishment. The interview was designed to examine those aspects of Watson and Crick's work which had led them to unravel the structure of DNA ahead of an array of other highly accomplished scientists.

At first, Watson listed a set of contributory factors that were largely unsurprising: it was crucial that he and Crick had identified the problem that was the most important to attack. They were both passionate about their work; they devoted themselves single-mindedly to the task at hand. They were willing to embrace approaches that were outside their area of familiarity. But then he added another reason for their success that was nothing short of stunning. He and Crick had cracked the elusive code for DNA primarily, he said, because they were *not* the most intelligent scientists pursuing the answer.

Say that again? How could it be, as Watson would go on to claim, that sometimes seeing yourself as the most intelligent decision-maker, the smartest individual present, could in fact be one of the most dangerous of all predicaments? Are there hidden perils to being the brightest person in the room?

Watson went on to explain in this interview that the most intelligent person working on the project at the time was Rosalind Franklin, a British scientist based in Paris at the time: 'Rosalind was so intelligent that she rarely sought advice. And if you're the brightest person in the room, then you're in trouble.'

Watson's comment sheds light on a familiar error seen in the actions of many well-intentioned leaders. Leaders in organisations who are dealing with a specific issue or problem – for example, how to design the most powerful sales pitch for a possible client, or the most effective campaign to raise funds for a parent–teacher association – should ensure that they collaborate with team members towards their goal, even if they are the best-informed, most experienced or most skilled person in the group. Not to do so might prove to be foolhardy. In fact, behavioural scientist Patrick Laughlin and his colleagues have shown that the approaches and outcomes of groups that cooperate in working towards a solution are not just better than those of the average member working alone, but are even better than those of the group's best problem-solver working alone. Far too often leaders who, by virtue of greater experience, skill and wisdom, deem themselves the ablest problem-solver in the group, fail to ask for input from team members.

The research conducted by Laughlin and his colleagues tells us why the best leader operating individually will be beaten to the solution by a less expert but cooperating unit. First, lone decision-makers can't match the diversity of knowledge and perspectives of a multi-person unit that includes them. The input from others can stimulate thinking processes that wouldn't have been developed when working alone. We can all recall being led to an insight by the comment of a colleague who didn't deliver the insight but who sparked the association. Second, the solution-seeker who goes it alone loses another significant advantage – the power of parallel processing. Whereas a cooperating unit can distribute many sub-tasks of a problem to its members, a lone operator must perform each task sequentially.

But isn't full collaboration risky? After all, decisions arrived at by committee are notorious for suboptimal performance. Mindful of that problem, our recommendation is not to employ a vote-counting strategy in order to reach a conclusion; in fact what we advise is not to make joint decisions at all. The final choice should always be for the leader to make. But it's the process of seeking input which leaders should engage in more collectively. And those who foster regular team input can expect not only to achieve better outcomes; in addition, they can expect closer relationships and rapport with their team, which enhances future collaboration and influence. But is there not a risk of bruised egos and lost motivation if a team member's idea is ultimately rejected? As long as a leader assures the team that each view – while perhaps not the deciding factor – will be considered in the process, this shouldn't arise. And who knows, although building a team of people who are encouraged to collaborate with each other may not enable you to declare, like Watson and Crick, that you have 'found the secret to life', it may well help you to find the secret to unlocking your and your group's true potential.

24

What can be learnt from captainitis?

Besides the dangers of *seeing yourself* as the best decision-maker in the room, there is another hazard that can be equally (if not more) perilous – being *seen by others* as the brightest or most experienced person in the room. This becomes critically important when that room is the cockpit of an aircraft, and the leader in question is its pilot.

Take, for example, the following exchange, from Air Florida Flight 90's flight recorder just before it fell into the icy Potomac river near Washington, DC, in 1982:

Co-pilot: Let's check the ice on those tops [wings] again since we've been sitting here a while.

Captain: No. I think we get to go in a minute.

Co-pilot: [Referring to an instrument as they prepare to take off] That doesn't seem right, does it? Uh, no that's not right.

Captain: Yes it is …

Co-pilot: Ah, maybe it is.

[*Sound of plane straining unsuccessfully to gain altitude*]

Co-pilot: Larry, we're going down.

Captain: I know it.

[*Sound of impact that killed captain, co-pilot and 76 others*]

This is but one tragic example of how members of a team often defer to the status of a leader as a legitimate and knowledgeable authority figure. It also shows how leaders often fail to see the influence that their perceived status and expertise has on those around them. Termed *captainitis*, this kind of behaviour gets its name from the sometimes deadly type of passivity displayed by crew members when a flight captain clearly makes an incorrect decision. Accident investigators have repeatedly recorded disastrous instances of an obvious error made by an airline captain that was not corrected by another crew member.

Captainitis isn't just limited to air travel. In one set of studies, researchers tested the willingness of qualified trained nurses to give up professional responsibilities towards a patient once the 'boss' of the case – the attending doctor – had spoken. To perform the experiment, psychological researcher Charles Hofling made a telephone call to 22 separate nurse stations on a variety of hospital wards. The caller identified himself as a hospital doctor and directed the nurse to give 20mg of the drug Astrogen to a specific patient. In 95 per cent of cases, the nurse went directly to the medicine cabinet to collect the drug and approached the patient to administer it even though the drug had not been cleared for hospital use and the 20mg prescription was twice that of the recommended daily dose.

Summarising their findings, the researchers made a telling point. They concluded that in fully staffed medical units, it's natural to assume that multiple 'professional intelligences' (doctors, nurses, pharmacists) are working together to ensure that the best decisions are made, but under closer scrutiny only one of those intelligences may be functioning. In this study it appears that the nurses abandoned their considerable experience and expertise and deferred to the doctor. In such a situation, the nurses' actions are understandable. The attending doctor is both *in authority* and *an authority*. In other words, the doctor is in charge, and as a result has the power to penalise non-compliant staff; and the doctor also possesses superior medical training which can lead those around him to defer to his or her expert status. As a result of this perceived expertise, we shouldn't be surprised when medical staff are reluctant to challenge a doctor's recommended treatment.

Leaders should be aware of these findings, not necessarily to protect themselves the next time they find themselves in a hospital, but the next time they find themselves in their office or a boardroom making an important decision. When leaders fail to ask for input from team members, and when team members fail to assert their opinions to leaders, it can become a vicious circle, leading to poor decision-making procedures, bad choices and often avoidable errors. Whether you're the coach of a sports team, an officer in a club, the owner of a small business or CEO of a multinational corporation, collaborative leadership, in which dissent from one's knowledgeable staff is invited, can be a key to breaking that cycle. And a little humility from leaders can't hurt either. Just remember to check your ego at the boardroom, hospital or cockpit door.

25

How can the nature of group meetings lead to unnatural disasters?

In space exploration, two days of national mourning have been etched into history for ever. On 1 February 2003, the US shuttle *Columbia* was destroyed upon re-entry into the earth's atmosphere; and on 28 January 1986 the US shuttle *Challenger* exploded during lift-off. Both disasters killed all seven crew members. Although the causes of each tragedy – in one case damage to the leading edge of the shuttle's left wing, and in the other a failed O-ring seal on the shuttle's solid rocket booster – were seemingly different, a close examination of these failures suggests the same root cause: NASA's poor decision-making culture. What lessons can be learnt from these tragedies, and how can we create a culture in our workplace which allows others to *persuade us* that we're wrong?

In order to first try to understand how these disasters came about, consider the following exchange between a *Columbia* disaster investigator and the chairwoman of the mission management team:

Investigator: As a manager, how do you seek out dissenting opinions?

Chairwoman: Well, when I hear about them …

Investigator: By their very nature, you may not have heard about them ... what techniques do you use to get them?

The chairwoman had no answer.

In the case of the *Columbia* disaster, managers ignored requests from lower-level staff to ask the Department of Defense to use its spy satellites to photograph potentially damaged areas of the shuttle. With *Challenger*, managers ignored warnings from the engineers that the cold weather on the day of the launch might cause the O-rings to fail. What factors can lead to such poor decision-making?

Examining real-world decision-making failures, such as Kennedy's Bay of Pigs invasion and Nixon's Watergate scandal, social psychologist Irving Janis developed a theory for how groups come to make poor decisions – 'groupthink', a term coined by journalist William H. Whyte. Groupthink is a kind of group decision-making style in which there's a greater need among members of the group to get along and agree with one another than to seek out and critically assess alternative views and ideas. It's often caused by a desire for group cohesiveness, isolation from outside influences, and authoritarian leaders who make their opinions known – factors that are present at various levels in many organisations. These factors often create a perceived pressure from others to conform to the leader's viewpoint. They can also lead to a perceived need to censor opposing views and keep the leaders shielded from such views, causing the false perceptions that group members completely agree with one another and that views expressed outside the group are inferior. The outcome is a defective discussion and decision-making process, often characterised by an incomplete survey of alternative ideas, a biased information search process and failure to assess the risks of the options favoured by the group's leaders.

What kind of steps can be taken to avoid such inferior decision-making? Group decision-making can be improved by promoting criticism and scepticism of all viewpoints, especially those favoured by the group's leaders. Astute leaders should always ask for the thoughts of others before they make their own positions known, thereby ensuring that they have access to a team's actual thoughts, opinions and insights rather than those that tell the leader what he or she wants to hear.

To employ this strategy effectively, leaders should promote an open and honest environment where individual opinions are welcomed and considered without fear of retribution. Most importantly, even after a decision has been made, the group should reconvene to discuss any doubts they may still have about the decision. Furthermore, it's often crucial to bring in outside experts, who will be less biased in their assessments of ideas. This should be especially effective when one considers that looking within an organisation is sometimes short-sighted, often leading teams to uncover what's already known within that culture. To get a better understanding of what's not known but could be useful and insightful requires an outside view.

In short, sometimes it's important to hear 'no' from your group to increase the likelihood that you'll hear 'yes' from those you're trying to persuade to adopt the group's decision.

26

Who is the better persuader? Devil's advocate or true dissenter?

For nearly four centuries, the Roman Catholic Church relied on the *advocatus diaboli*, or devil's advocate, to investigate and to present to the Church all the negative aspects of the life and work of a candidate for sainthood. In what might be viewed as a form of saintly due diligence, the idea was that by uncovering all the unfavourable information concerning the candidate and presenting it to the Church leadership, the decision-making process would be more informed and would benefit considerably from the diversity of ideas, perspectives and sources of information.

Anyone who works in the business world knows that the terms 'business' and 'sainthood' are not common companions. Yet business managers could learn a valuable lesson from the devil's advocate procedure. When it seems that everyone on a team initially agrees on an issue it can often be fruitful to *encourage* alternative points of view. This becomes even more important when you consider the potentially devastating effects of groupthink and group polarisation, in which the majority opinion in a group becomes more extreme the more it is discussed.

Social psychologists have also known for some time that even one lone dissenter in an otherwise unanimous group may be enough to generate more creative and complex thinking within that group. But until recently, very little research had been conducted into the nature of the dissenter. Are devil's advocates – i.e. pseudo-dissenters – better or worse than authentic dissenters at enhancing the problem-solving abilities of a group of otherwise like-minded people?

The results of a study conducted by social psychologist Charlan Nemeth and colleagues suggest that, in comparison with an authentic dissenter, a person asked to play the role of devil's advocate will be much less effective at promoting creative problem-solving among group members. The researchers argue that majority members are more likely to perceive the true dissenter's arguments and positions as principled, and therefore as valid. The stance of the devil's advocate, on the other hand, seems like disagreement simply for the sake of disagreement. When the majority members are confronted by a person who truly appears to oppose their position, they try to understand why the dissenter is so committed to his or her beliefs. In the process, they come to a better understanding of the problem and consider it from a broader perspective.

Do these findings imply that the devil's advocate is obsolete? In the 1980s, Pope John Paul II officially terminated their use in Catholic Church practice. Indeed, there's some evidence that experience with a devil's advocate has the potential to *strengthen*, rather than weaken, majority members' confidence in their original position, presumably because they believe that they have considered – and subsequently dismissed – all possible alternatives. This isn't to say that there's no benefit to the devil's advocate, however. They may be useful in calling attention to alternative ideas, perspectives and information, as long as the majority considers these alternatives with an open mind.

But considering the findings of this research, perhaps the

best policy for leaders is to create and sustain a work environment in which co-workers and subordinates are encouraged to openly disagree with the majority viewpoint. This could well translate into more innovative solutions to complex problems and higher employee morale (as long as dissension remains professional and not personal), and could eventually lead to increased profits. In situations where decisions will have long-lasting and potentially far-reaching implications, consideration should also be given to actually seeking out true dissenters. By encouraging knowledgeable others to passionately persuade us that we may be leaning in the wrong direction, we place ourselves in a position where we gain a greater understanding from a genuine argument rather than a simulated one, allowing us to make optimal decisions and create maximally effective messages.

27

When can the right way be the wrong way?

Strength. Courage. Determination. Commitment. Selflessness. Some might say that our firefighters should be role models for how we should behave both inside and outside our organisations. Even though saving lives and rescuing kittens from trees might not be in your job description, learning how firefighters train for their job might just help you become an everyday hero in yours.

Behavioural researcher Wendy Joung and her colleagues were interested in examining whether certain types of training programmes would be more effective than others at minimising errors in judgement on the job. Specifically, they wanted to know whether focusing the trainee on past errors that others had made would provide better training than focusing the trainee on how others made good decisions in the past. They thought that training that focused more on others' errors would be more effective owing to several factors, including increased attention paid and a more memorable experience.

The researchers aimed to test their hypothesis on a group of people whose decision-making skills under stress were vital, and whose decisions carried important consequences; so it's not surprising they chose firefighters. In the study, a training and development session that included several case studies was presented to the firefighters. The nature of the case studies differed, however, between two groups of participants. One group learned from case studies that described real-life situations in which other firefighters made poor decisions that led to negative outcomes. The other group learned from case studies in which firefighters avoided negative outcomes through good decision-making. When the researchers analysed the data, they found greater improvements in the judgement of the firefighters who underwent the error-based training compared with those who underwent the error-free training.

Training is all about influencing others, so if you want to maximise your influence on employees' future behaviours, the implications for your organisation's training programmes are clear. Although many companies typically focus their training exclusively on the positive – in other words, on how to make good decisions – the results of this study suggest that a sizeable portion of the training should be devoted to how others have made errors in the past and how those errors could have been (and can be) avoided. Specifically, case studies, videos, illustrations and personal testimonials covering the mistakes should be followed by a discussion of what actions would have been appropriate to take in these and similar situations.

Of course, specific individuals don't have to be singled out by management for their previous poor decision-making, as these error-based experiences could be completely anonymous. You might find, however, that some of the more experienced and respected employees are more than happy to donate their error-laden 'war stories' to the company's training archive.

This approach shouldn't be limited to the corporate classroom. Teachers, sports coaches and just about anyone who provides training to others can benefit from such a strategy – including parents, of course. For example, when teaching their children to stay away from strangers, parents can describe hypothetical scenarios in which a child got tricked by a stranger. By focusing on what the child in the example could have done to get away from the stranger in that specific situation, he or she will be better prepared to deal with such scenarios in the future.

28

What's the best way to turn a weakness into a strength?

Nearly half a century ago, the advertising firm of Doyle, Dane, & Bernbach was challenged with the almost insurmountable task of introducing a tiny German automobile to a US market in which only larger domestic cars had previously thrived. Within a short period, the Volkswagen Beetle was transformed from a relatively obscure laughing-stock into a popular status symbol. The success of the Beetle can be largely attributed to the firm's engineering of one of the greatest campaigns in the history of advertising. Perhaps most astonishing is how the firm set about this task: when promoting the brand, they didn't emphasise the product's strengths, such as its relative cheapness or its modest fuel consumption. Instead, they touted its weaknesses. Why?

The advertising campaign certainly broke with the industry's conventional wisdom at the time. It focused on the fact that the Volkswagen was not nearly as pleasing to the eye as the typical American-made cars of the day. The types of strapline featured in these ads were slogans such as 'Ugly is only skin deep' and 'It will stay uglier longer'. It's easy to understand why these straplines attracted attention, and to see why the campaign overall was very likeable. But these factors alone can't account for the huge surge in sales that accompanied the launch and whole career of this campaign. How did these advertisements succeed in selling so many cars?

Mentioning a small drawback of a product creates the perception that the company advertising the product is honest and trustworthy. That puts the company in a position to be more persuasive when promoting the product's genuine strengths – in the case of the Beetle, as mentioned, modest fuel consumption and an affordable price. Similarly, Avis, the world's *second*-largest car rental company, took advantage of this principle in their memorable motto 'Avis. We're #2, but we try harder. (When you're not #1, you have to.)'. Other examples include 'Listerine: The taste you hate three times a day' and 'L'Oréal: We're expensive, but you're worth it'.

Evidence for the success of this strategy has been found outside the domain of advertising as well. Consider one example of its use in law: in a study conducted by behavioural scientist Kip Williams and colleagues, when jurors heard a lawyer mention a weakness in his own case before the opposing attorney mentioned it, they rated him as more trustworthy and were more favourable to his overall case in their verdicts because of that perceived honesty. Additionally, anyone who is considering a career change may be interested to learn that a recruitment study found that applicants whose curriculum vitae contained only wholly positive references were invited to fewer interviews than those whose curriculum vitae first highlighted a weakness or slight limitation before going on to describe positive characteristics.

There are a number of other applications for this persuasion technique. For example, if you're selling your car, when a prospective buyer comes to give it a test drive, volunteering negative information about the car, especially of a kind that the prospect would be unlikely to discover on his or her own (e.g.

the light inside the boot is a little dodgy or the fuel economy is modest), should do wonders for his or her trust in you and your vehicle.

The strategy can also be applied at the negotiating table. For example, if there's a small area in which your leverage is weak, your negotiating partner is likely to see you as more trustworthy if you mention it up front rather than leaving it to be discovered later. The same goes for direct sales: if you are selling colour copiers to a business, and your copier holds slightly less paper than your competitors', it might be helpful to mention that fact early on in the process to earn the potential buyer's trust. Then it would be easier to convince the buyer that the truly superior features of your copier really do surpass the competition in those areas.

Note, however, that you're only going to be able to use this strategy effectively if most of your weaknesses are genuinely minor ones. This is why we rarely see ad campaigns with mottos like 'Ranked last in its class by J. D. Power and Associates, but once we get these wrongful death suits taken care of, we'll try harder'.

29

Which faults unlock people's vaults?

François, Duc de La Rochefoucauld, the seventeenth-century French writer and moralist, foreshadowed the astonishing success of the famed VW Beetle advertising campaign when he wrote, 'We only confess our little faults to persuade people that we have no big ones.' Although that campaign seemed to handle its product's faults deftly, attempting to use these types of messages leaves us with a dilemma: *which* little faults should we choose to confess?

Research conducted by social scientist Gerd Bohner and his colleagues suggests that for such 'two-sided' persuasive appeals to be maximally effective, there must be a clear connection between the negative and positive attributes that are conveyed. In one study, Bohner created three different versions of an advertisement for a restaurant. One message featured only positive attributes. To take just one example, the advertisement touted the restaurant's cosy atmosphere. A second message mentioned those positive features in addition to some unrelated negative ones. For example, in addition to mentioning the cosy atmosphere, the advertisement stated that the restaurant couldn't offer dedicated parking. The third message described certain negative features and added some related positive ones. For instance, the ad described the restaurant as very small, but it also mentioned that it had a cosy atmosphere.

So, participants who saw the third advertisement were able to make the connection between the negative aspects of the restaurant and the positive ones ('There's little space, but that's part of what makes the atmosphere cosy'). In short, although both types of two-sided messages produced increases in the restaurant owner's perceived credibility, the evaluation of the restaurant was highest after the two-sided message in which the positive and negative attributes were related.

These findings indicate that if you're primarily looking to increase your trustworthiness in the eyes of others, the particular types of weaknesses you convey in your two-sided messages are less likely to matter. If, however, you're also looking to enhance their positive feelings towards the object of discussion – be it a restaurant, a product or even your credentials – then you'd be well advised to ensure that any dark cloud you describe is paired with a silver lining tailored to that cloud. To take a real-life example, when US president Ronald Reagan was up for re-election in 1984, some voters were concerned that he was too old for an effective second term. During the presidential debate against opponent Walter Mondale, Reagan acknowledged that he was very old, but stated: 'I want you to know that also I will not make age an issue of this campaign. I am not going to exploit for political purposes my opponent's youth and inexperience.' Although Mondale's immediate response was to let out a laugh, he was certainly not laughing when he was later routed in one of the biggest landslide in US presidential history.

This research has many business applications, as well. For instance, let's say that you're presenting a product that your company has recently launched to a new client. It has some notable features and benefits over that of your competitors, but they come at a price. As a result, it costs some 20 per cent more than the product that this new client company is currently using. You also know, however, that this initial 20 per cent premium is offset by the fact that your product lasts longer and is more cost-effective to maintain. It's also faster and more compact, using up significantly less space than your competitors'.

The results of this research suggest that after you mention the weakness of the price premium, you should follow that statement with a benefit related to cost and not to any other attribute of your product. A statement such as 'On the face of it, our new product has a twenty per cent price premium, but this is more than offset when you consider how much longer it lasts and the lower maintenance costs' would be more persuasive than a statement such as 'On the face of it, our new product has a twenty per cent price premium, but it's much faster and also takes up less space'.

In other words, be sure to follow your discussion of a drawback with a virtue that's related to, and neutralises, the drawback. When fate gives us lemons, we should try to make lemonade, not apple juice.

30 When is it right to admit that you were wrong?

In February 2007, JetBlue Airways, the New York-based low-cost American airline, frustrated thousands of passengers because of a lack of preparation and poor decision-making in the face of severe winter weather in the north-eastern United States. Almost without exception, all other airlines that provided passenger service in that region had cancelled massive numbers of flights in anticipation of the storm. In contrast, JetBlue gave hope to many of its passengers that their planes would fly. The storms didn't let up, however, so many of JetBlue's customers were let down.

After stranding thousands of passengers in airports and on tarmacs in this operational nightmare, JetBlue faced a difficult public relations decision: who or what to blame? Should they point to external factors, like the extreme weather, or should they focus the blame on internal factors relevant to the company's operations? The company chose the latter, acknowledging that JetBlue's failures during the meltdown were caused by internal rather than external problems. It takes bravery and a sense of humility to admit one's mistakes, which is perhaps why it is so rare to see organisations and the people within them take the blame for a misstep or a misjudgement. Does the social influence research support the decision by JetBlue to do what many companies in their position would probably never even consider?

Social scientist Fiona Lee and her colleagues suggest that organisations that attribute failures to internal causes will come out ahead not only in public perception, but also in terms of the profit line. They argue that blaming internal, potentially controllable failures makes the organisation appear as if it has greater control over its own resources and future. They also suggest that the public response might be to assume that the organisation has a plan to modify the features that may have led to the problems in the first place.

To test these ideas, Lee and colleagues conducted a brief study in which participants read one of two annual reports of a fictitious company, both of which explained why the company had performed so poorly over the last year. For half of the participants, the annual report blamed internal (but potentially controllable) factors for the poor performance:

Fictitious company report A

The unexpected drop in earnings this year is primarily attributable to some of the strategic decisions we made last year. Decisions to acquire a new company and to push out several new drugs in international markets directly contributed to short-term decreases in earnings. As a management team, we were not fully prepared for the unfavourable conditions that emerged from both the domestic and international sectors.

For the other half of the participants, the annual report blamed external (and uncontrollable) factors for the poor performance:

Fictitious company report B

The drop in earnings this year is primarily attributable to the unexpected downturn in the domestic and international economic environment and increased international competition. These unfavourable market conditions directly contributed to a short-term slump in sales and difficulties in the introduction of several key drugs to the market. These unexpected conditions arose from federal legislations and are completely outside our control.

Participants who saw Report A viewed the company more positively on a number of different dimensions than did participants who saw Report B.

But the researchers didn't stop there – they wanted to test their hypothesis in a real-life setting. To do this, they collected hundreds of these types of statements from the annual reports of fourteen companies over a 21-year period. They discovered that when these companies explained failures in their annual reports, those that pointed to internal and controllable factors had higher stock prices one year later than those that pointed to external and uncontrollable factors. So, if taking responsibility for your mistakes and admitting that you're wrong is not only the right thing to do but also right for your company, why is this behaviour such a rarity? Often the response to a costly or embarrassing error, regardless of who made it, whether an organisation or an individual, is to attempt to blame external persons or factors to divert attention from the source of the problem. By taking such an approach, we create two bigger problems for ourselves. First, as the research suggests, this strategy is likely to be ineffective because it does nothing to prove to sceptics that we have control of the problem and the ability to fix it. Second, even if we do manage to distract attention away from our mistake in the short term, the spotlight – or perhaps more accurately the bull's-eye – will find its way back to us in the long term, potentially highlighting not only our mistake but also our deceptive impulses.

This should hold true not only for companies, but also for individuals. If you find yourself in a situation in which you've made a mistake, you should admit it, and follow up immediately with an action plan demonstrating that you can take control of the situation and put it right. Through these actions, you'll ultimately put yourself in a position of greater influence by being perceived as not only capable, but also honest.

In sum, the results of this research suggest that if you play the blame game – pointing your finger at external factors rather than at yourself – both you and your organisation will be likely to end up as the losers.

31

When should you be pleased that the server is down?

Computer glitches have the power to make your work environment a frustrating place to do business. Recent research, however, suggests that there are certain cases in which computer glitches can actually be a boon rather than a bane to your business.

Social scientists Charles Naquin and Terri Kurtzberg had the idea that when organisations identify technology – as opposed to human error – as the main cause of an incident, customers and other outsiders will be less likely to hold the organisation as a whole responsible. To test this hypothesis, accounting students in one study were asked to read a fictitious newspaper article that was based on a real accident that occurred between two Chicago Transit Authority commuter trains, in which scores were injured and many more were inconvenienced. Half of the participants were told that the problem was due to a technological error. Specifically, they were informed that there was an error in the train's computer program which caused it to move forward when the correct course of action was to stop. The other half of the participants were told that the problem was due to human error – the train's conductor simply let the train move forward when it should have been stopped. The researchers found that the participants assigned less blame to the Chicago

Transit Authority when told that its technological errors caused the accident.

In another study, the researchers took advantage of a real incident that occurred on a university campus. During the incident, the university's e-mail system allowed users only to e-mail campus addresses, a problem that lasted for a full work day. The researchers handed out surveys to MBA students asking them the extent to which they believed that the Office of Information Technology (OIT), which managed the university's computer network, should be held accountable for this disruption. Before responding to the survey, half of the MBA students were told that the disruption was 'believed to be the result of a computer error that consequently fried the server', whereas the other half were told that the disruption was 'believed to be the result of human error that consequently fried the server'. The results revealed that participants assigned greater blame to the OIT, including suggesting more substantial financial penalties, when they believed the disruption was caused by human error rather than by technological error.

Why? The results of the study suggest that when people learn the cause of an organisation's problem, they think of how avoidable it was; and accidents caused by human error simply produce more of these thoughts than those with technological causes, owing probably to the perception of greater control for incidents associated with human foul-ups.

As we discussed in the previous chapter, most of us are naturally inclined to downplay or even hide mistakes that have occurred, especially when the issue could have a negative impact on one of our customers or colleagues. But when confronted with such evasions, those affected by the incident may well assume that the problem was caused by human errors that could easily have been avoided. And although we've advocated accepting the blame when you or your organisation makes mistakes, in cases in which the problems are truly due to technological glitches rather than human error, people should make all relevant others aware of this small but important piece of information. Just be sure to make it clear that you have pinpointed the problem, which signals that you have control over the situation and are able to prevent its recurrence.

Delays due to technological problems seem to be an ever-increasing problem in our everyday lives. In fact, it's estimated that the average UK citizen will spend upwards of eighteen hours a year held up in delays caused by technical difficulties on public transport, which is equivalent to over 55 days in a person's lifetime. Although delays of any sort can be a frustrating part of life, what can often be even more infuriating is the lack of information as to the cause of the delay. So, if you find yourself in the unenviable position of having to announce a problem or delay that's rooted in technical difficulties, you should present the information as quickly as possible to those affected by the problem. By doing so, you'll be effective in two ways. First, you'll present yourself as helpful, informative and on their side. And second, you'll make it clear that you know the source of the foul-up and will therefore have more control in the future.

32

How can similarities make a difference?

In the summer of 1993, the flood waters of the Mississippi river threatened to devastate several cities in the Midwest, including the city of Quincy, Illinois. In response to the imminent danger, hundreds of Quincy residents worked night and day to secure vulnerable areas with thousands of sandbags. Things looked bleak for the residents; supplies and sources of food were steadily declining while fatigue, pessimism and, worst of all, the water levels were on the rise. The mood among the volunteers brightened considerably, however, when they learned that residents of a small city in Massachusetts had donated a large amount of provisions, that were already en route.

What was it that influenced the people of a seemingly random city to act so generously towards a town located 1,000 miles away? And why help Quincy in particular, as opposed to any of the many other cities and towns that were threatened by flood waters?

A substantial amount of psychological research has shown that we're most likely to follow the behaviour of others with whom we share personal characteristics, such as values, beliefs, age and gender. But the answer to this particular question lies in a subtle and seemingly irrelevant similarity between the two municipalities. Simply on the basis of a shared name, the residents of Quincy, Massachusetts, felt a bond with the people of Quincy, Illinois, that was strong enough to motivate their generosity.

What can explain this? Social psychologists have found that we tend to feel especially positive towards some subtle things that are associated with ourselves, such as our names. This tendency has manifested itself in some surprisingly powerful ways. Evidence suggests, for example, that people are more likely to comply with a stranger's request when the two have the same birthday.

In another set of studies, researcher Randy Garner sent surveys to perfect strangers by mail. Accompanying the survey was a request to complete and return it made by a person whose name was either similar or dissimilar to the name of the survey recipient. For example, in the similar name condition, a person whose name was Robert Greer might get the survey from someone named Bob Gregar or a woman named Cynthia Johnston might get the survey from someone named Cindy Johanson. The names used in the not-similar condition were one of five names of the research assistants involved in the study.

Those who received the survey from someone with a similar-sounding name were nearly twice as likely to fill out and return the package as those who received the surveys from names that were not similar (56 per cent compared to 30 per cent). Moreover, after the first phase of the study was completed, all who had returned the original survey were sent another survey assessing what role various factors might have played in their decision to return the packet. For this survey, roughly half responded, but none of the participants indicated that the name of the sender affected their decision to complete the survey. Findings such as these show both the power and the subtlety of similarity as a cue that people take to decide whom to help.

One implication of these and similar social psychological findings is that potential clients may be more receptive to a pitch from a salesperson with whom they share similarities in any number of domains, including names, beliefs, home towns and alma maters. Pointing out similarities can also be the first step to resolving potentially ugly conflicts with co-workers and even neighbours. Of course, we're not advocating that people invent characteristics or attributes shared with others to gain their compliance. But what we are suggesting is that if you do share genuine similarities with someone, you should bring them to the surface in your discussions before making your request or presentation.

33

When is your name your game?

In one episode of the American adaptation of the British television comedy *The Office*, branch manager Michael Scott discovers that his sycophantic underling, Dwight Schrute, has gone behind his back to try to convince upper management to award Michael's job to him. To cover up his absence at work, Dwight tells Michael that he needs to go to the dentist to have a crown put in. When Dwight returns to the office, Michael asks him about his experience at the dentist. Unaware that Michael has learned about the coup attempt, Dwight tries to bluff:

Michael: Hey, I thought you weren't supposed to eat anything for a couple hours after you've had a crown put in?'

Dwight: [munching on candy] … They have this new kind of quick-drying bonding.

Michael: Oh? Sounds like a good dentist.

Dwight: Oh, yeah.

Michael: What's his name?

Dwight: [long pause] Crentist.

Michael: Your dentist's name is Crentist?

Dwight: Yeah.

Michael: Huh … sounds a lot like dentist.

Dwight: Maybe that's why he became a dentist.

Although Dwight's explanation of how 'Dr Crentist' became attracted to the profession of dentistry sounds ridiculous, if not completely idiotic, new research makes it clear that claims like Dwight's might actually have a basis in reality. In the previous chapter, we discussed how people tend to have more positive feelings towards – and are more likely to comply with requests from – others who are similar to themselves in some way, even in superficial ways like having similar-sounding names. But is it possible that our names can affect important, life-altering decisions, such as the type of career we decide to pursue or where we decide to live?

Research conducted by behavioural scientist Brett Pelham and his colleagues suggests that the answer is yes. They claim that the tendency to favour things we associate with our names does in fact have a subtle but powerful influence on major life decisions. According to the researchers, there's a reason why Susie chose a job in which she could sell seashells by the seashore and why Peter Piper went for a profession picking pecks of pickled peppers, not the other way around: people are attracted to professions with names similar to their own.

To test this idea, Pelham came up with a list of names that sounded like the word *dentist*, such as Dennis. According to census data, the name Dennis was the 40th most frequent male first name in the US population at the time, with the names Jerry and Walter ranking 39th and 41st respectively. Armed with this information, Pelham searched the national directory of the American Dental Association, examining the number of dentists with one of those three first names. If people's names have no effect whatsoever on what career path they follow, you'd expect that there should be roughly equal numbers of people with these three names going into the field of dentistry.

But that's not what Pelham and his colleagues found. The

nationwide search revealed that 257 dentists were named Walter, 270 were named Jerry and 482 were named Dennis. That means that dentists are about 82 per cent more likely to be named Dennis than you'd expect if name similarity had absolutely no effect on career choice. Similarly, people whose names begin with *Geo* (e.g. George, Geoffrey) are disproportionately likely to do research in the geosciences (e.g. geology). In fact, even just the first letter of a person's name influences his or her career choice. For example, they found that hardware store owners are around 80 per cent more likely to have names that start with the letter *H* than with the letter *R*, but roofers are about 70 per cent more likely to have names that start with *R* than with *H*. Of course, if you were to ask, say, a thousand roofers whose names begin with *R* whether their names played any role at all in the career they chose, it's likely that half of them would see you as crazy and the other half as stupid.*

It turns out that the tendency to be drawn to things that are associated with ourselves plays out in other important areas of life, including where we decide to live. To cite just a few of their findings, Pelham and his colleague have shown that, at a disproportionate rate:

▓ People move to states that are similar to their own names. For example, people called Florence are disproportionately likely to move to Florida, and people named Louise are disproportionately likely to move to Louisiana.

▓ People move to cities with numbers in them that match

---

* This fact was highlighted at a recent conference where one of the authors was speaking. Keen to point out a situation where there was no similarity between a person's name and career, a delegate commented, 'I have a friend named Dennis and he's not a dentist.' When asked by another delegate what Dennis did in fact do for a living, he let out a huge sigh and said, 'Actually, he's a demolition worker.'

their own birthdate numbers. For example, cities with the number 2 in their names, such as Two Harbors, Minnesota, have a disproportionate number of residents who were born on 2 February (2/2), whereas cities that have the number 3 in their names, such as Three Forks, Montana, have a disproportionate number of residents who were born on 3 March (3/3).

■ People choose to live on streets whose names match their own. In other words, someone named Mr Washington is more likely to choose to live on Washington Street than someone named Mr Jefferson.

■ People choose to marry others who have similar-sounding first or last names. All else being roughly equal, if Eric, Erica, Charles and Charlotte all meet one another for the first time, Erica will be more likely to become romantically involved with Eric than with Charles, and the opposite is more likely to occur with Charlotte.

■ When asked to trust their feelings and intuitions, people prefer products whose first letters match the first letters of their own name. So someone named Arielle might be more likely to put the chocolate bar Aero towards the top of her list than someone named Larry, who might be more likely to favour a Lion Bar.

For companies naming new products aimed at a mass market, this research may suggest only that they should avoid names that start with uncommon letters, such as *Z*, *X* and *Q*. But if you're designing a programme, initiative or product that's being tailored for a specific client, you can harness the power of people's natural tendency to be attracted to things that remind them of themselves, in the name that you give it. Specifically, you should base the title on the client's name or even just the first letter of his or her name. For example, if you're considering pitching a strategy to Pepsi, calling it the Pepsi Proposal or even something like the Peterson Plan would be more likely to be effective. And as long as the programme is truly customised for a particular client, the strategy should not only be successful but also completely costless.

Similarly, if you're having difficulty getting your child interested in reading books, finding one that has some name commonality with him or her (e.g. Harold or Harriet could be offered Harry Potter) might just be the key to getting them excited about it. Or if little Craig or Crystal is deathly afraid of paying a visit to the dentist, you could always look in the Yellow Pages to see whether you can find one named Crentist …

34

What tip should we take from those who get them?

From business lunches with clients to bonding experiences with our friends and family, restaurants play a vital role in the success of our professional and personal lives. Although there's quite a bit to be gained by interacting with our dining partners in such a setting, one great tip you get from a restaurant visit might just come from a different group of people – a group that hopes to get great tips all day, but is seldom asked to dish any out.

That group is waiters, who can teach us a great deal about how to be more persuasive. To take one example, many food servers have found that they receive larger tips when they repeat their customers' orders back to them exactly as the customer said. Many of us have had the experience of a waiter or waitress taking our order and then passively saying, 'OK,' or, worse still, not even acknowledging our order. It's perhaps not surprising that we prefer the service of someone who doesn't leave us wondering whether the cheeseburger we ordered will arrive at our table transformed into a chicken sandwich.

A piece of research by Rick van Baaren tested the idea that food servers who match their customers' verbalisations after receiving the order will increase their tip size. No paraphrasing, no nodding, no 'OKs' – just repeating back word for word the customer's order. In one study, simply by matching their customers' verbalisations after receiving the order, the food servers at one restaurant increased their tip size by nearly 70 per cent.

Why should mirroring another person elicit such a generous response from that person? Perhaps it ties into our natural inclination to prefer people who are similar to us. In fact, researchers Tanya Chartrand and John Bargh argue that matching the behaviours of others creates feelings of liking and strengthens bonds between two people. In one experiment, the researchers set up a situation in which two people had a brief interaction. One of the participants, however, was actually a research assistant. In half the cases, the research assistant mirrored the posture and behaviours of the other participant. In other words, if the participant sat cross-armed and tapped her foot, the research assistant sat cross-armed and tapped her foot. In the other half of cases, the research assistant didn't follow suit.

The researchers found that the participants who had been mirrored liked the research assistant more and felt that the interaction was smoother than did participants whose behaviour had not been mirrored. Similarly, food servers who match their customers' verbalisations probably garnered more tips because of the liking principle – that we want to do nice things for and say 'yes' to people we like.

Recently, researcher William Maddux and his colleagues conducted a set of experiments examining these processes in a different domain: negotiation. They suggested that behaviour-mirroring during negotiations could produce better outcomes not only for the person matching the other's behaviours, but for both parties. For example, in one experiment, MBA students were instructed either to subtly mirror their partner (e.g. lean back in your chair if the other person does) during a negotiation or not to mirror that person. When one party was instructed to mirror the other, the two parties reached a deal 67 per cent of the time. When they weren't told to mirror the other? Only a paltry 12.5 per cent. Based on some additional data from the experiment, the researchers concluded that behaviour-mirroring led to increased trust, and that increased trust typically led one negotiator to feel comfortable disclosing details that were ultimately necessary to break a stalemate and create a win–win situation.

You may well have had the experience of being in a meeting with a team member or negotiating with an adversary, and noticing that your posture is mirroring theirs. A typical response to this realisation is to change your physical positioning so that it no longer mirrors the other person's – in other words, you act as if there were something wrong with behaviour matching. This research suggests the exact opposite: the mirroring should result in *better* outcomes for you both, or at the very least the benefit to you won't come at the expense of the other person.

There are other applications of these findings. For example, if you work in sales and customer service settings, you can foster greater rapport with your clientele by first repeating customers' verbalisations back to them, regardless of whether those verbalisations are in the form of questions, complaints or even orders (e.g. 'So you're saying you'd *like to purchase ten units now with the possibility of increasing that to twenty units in May*').

The insight from this research was demonstrated in a less than desirable way when one of us was recently asked to review a series of recorded telephone conversations made to a customer services centre. One rather irate customer called and demanded to speak to a manager because she was angry about a particular promise that this company had failed to act on.

'I'm sorry you're upset,' came the reply from the customer service operator.

'I'm not upset, I'm angry,' replied the customer in an increasingly loud voice.

'Yes, I can hear that you are disturbed.'

'Disturbed? Disturbed? I am not disturbed, I am angry,' shouted the customer.

The conversation quickly spiralled into a battle of wills, with the customer becoming increasingly angry at the reluctance to acknowledge the fact that she was angry. The simple repetition of the customer's own words might have led to a different outcome. 'I'm sorry to hear that you are angry. What can we do together to resolve the situation?' would have been a better response and one that every one of us could apply to good effect when attempting to build better rapport and relationships.

The moral of this story? We can learn a lot about influencing others by observing how food servers interact with their customers. People say that imitation is the highest form of flattery, but these strategies indicate that imitation is also one of the most basic forms of persuasion.

35
What kind of smile can make the world smile back?

'**Don't open a shop unless** you like to smile,' warns a simple but instructive Chinese proverb. We've all heard about the importance of service with a smile, but is one smile the same as the next? Could the way you smile have a positive effect on those who see it?

Social scientist Alicia Grandey and her colleagues asked whether all types of smiles are equally effective when it comes to customer satisfaction. Based on previous findings demonstrating that people can often distinguish between authentic and inauthentic smiles, the research team thought that the authenticity of customer service workers' smiles could have an influence on customer satisfaction, even though the difference between the two types of smiles is very subtle.

In one study designed to test this possibility, the researchers had participants watch one of several videos of a conversation between an employee at the front desk of a hotel and a guest checking in; participants were asked to indicate how satisfied they would feel with the interaction had they been the guest. Unbeknown to the participants, the video was staged – the researchers hired actors to play the employee and the guest. Although the script between the actors remained the same, the researcher varied the instructions given to the actress playing the employee. In one case, she was asked to generate positive feelings towards the guest and to think about how she could make the guest feel good – the authentic condition. In the other case, she was told she was required to smile during the interaction – the inauthentic condition. The researchers also varied whether the hotel employee performed the tasks well or poorly. The first finding is an obvious one: the observers registered greater satisfaction when the hotel employee performed the tasks well compared with when they did poorly. A second finding was that when the tasks were performed poorly, the authenticity of the smile didn't make much of a difference in reported satisfaction. When the tasks were performed well, however, those who viewed the 'authentic smile' video said they would be more satisfied with the customer service than those who viewed the 'inauthentic smile' video.

In a second study, one that took place in a more natural setting, the researchers surveyed random restaurant patrons about how satisfied they were with the service of the waiting staff. The patrons were also asked about the perceived authenticity of the food servers' positive attitudes towards them. Consistent with the results of the other study, patrons who perceived their food servers to be authentic in their positive displays were more satisfied with their service.

The results of this research suggest a revision to the old adage 'Smile and the world smiles with you'. If you fake your smile, those you deal with may very well frown back. So how can we have, and encourage others to have, more authentically positive experiences?

One possibility for managers of service-oriented companies might be to provide emotional skills training to workers to help them better regulate and elevate their moods. After all, unhappy employees, when forced to smile for their customers, may engage in lower-quality interactions, which will ultimately lead to reduced customer satisfaction. But that kind of emotional training often requires a great deal of time and money.

A second, more general approach that we can all take is to try to follow the wisdom of Benjamin Franklin: 'Search others for their virtues'. Many of us spend too much time finding faults in the people we deal with. If, instead, we try to search their character for what we like about them, we'll like them more; and, as a result, they'll like us more. In short, everyone comes out ahead. This approach can even be fruitful in dealing with our superiors. As an example, one of us has a friend who had a very difficult relationship with her boss. They rarely saw eye to eye, but it was more than that – she truly disliked him as a person. One day, however, she decided that she was going to follow Franklin's advice. Even though her manager was not a kind person within the confines of the office, he was a very devoted family man, a trait that she genuinely admired. After focusing on this quality, a little at a time, she started to like him more and more. One day, she told him that she admired how family-oriented he was, which she could say quite honestly. To her surprise, the next day he was in her office, giving her a heads-up on some information that was very useful to her – an action she's certain he never would have taken otherwise.

36

Immediately after the announcement of the death of Pope John Paul II on the evening of 2 April 2005, a strange thing happened. Without any apparent explanation, hordes of people began entering souvenir shops and buying up all manner of commemorative items such as coffee cups and silver spoons. Now, such behaviour would be instantly explicable if these people were taking the opportunity to buy a small trinket or item that featured the face of John Paul II, to own a souvenir that commemorated his reign as head of the Catholic Church. But these souvenirs didn't feature the recently deceased pope. In fact, the stampede didn't even occur in the Vatican City or Rome or even Italy, for that matter. It occurred well over a thousand miles away, but there can be no doubting the influence that the pope's death had on these curious buying behaviours.

Often credited as a notable force in the fall of communism, Pope John Paul II also had a significant influence over issues from consumerism to abortion ... but commemorative coffee cups? Not just any commemorative coffee cups, but royal ones to be precise, commemorating the wedding of Charles, Prince of Wales, to Camilla Parker Bowles, held on Friday, 8 April 2005 in Windsor, England. In fact, it wasn't just coffee cups which attracted a rush of sales. Tea services, silver spoons, tea towels, mouse mats and key rings were the target for many a souvenir hunter. What could cause such a remarkable stampede?

On Monday, 4 April 2005 the Vatican City announced that the funeral service for Pope John Paul II would take place in Rome on the following Friday – the same day on which the royal wedding was scheduled. As a mark of respect, and in order for the Prince of Wales to attend the funeral, the royal family hastily rearranged the wedding, which would now take place the day after the funeral, on Saturday, 9 April 2005. As a result, every souvenir shop in Windsor now had stocks of commemorative wedding souvenirs marked with the wrong date. Spotting a potential opportunity to make financial gains, people began to buy up all the misdated souvenirs, invariably thinking that they could sell these soon-to-be scarce commodities at a later date, perhaps on eBay or to an interested collector.

The misdated souvenirs became a modern-day misprinted Penny Black. And as word got out of the purchase of the misdated souvenirs, this served only to increase the number of souvenir hunters. The shops soon sold out. A number of journalists who were already in Windsor preparing to cover the story of the royal wedding stopped people as they left the shops armed with their bags of souvenirs and asked whether they were the type of person who would ordinarily buy these things. To their surprise, the majority answered no. These souvenir hunters weren't being influenced by the need for a coffee mug or the quality of the product or even its connection to a royal event. They were persuaded by the fact that it was misdated and as a result might be worth something in the future.

During the past five decades scientific studies of persuasion have concluded time and time again that rare and unique items hold greater value for us. We want things more when we learn that they are scarce, available only in limited quantities and for a limited time. In the case of the royal souvenirs people probably assumed that the shop owners would throw away the misdated items by the truckload because of the incorrect information. Ironic, then, that as the wedding wasn't one of the more popular royal events of recent times, a couple of days later, when shops restocked with souvenirs featuring the revised date of the wedding, more people owned the misdated souvenirs than the ones with the right date. The misdated souvenirs, while assumed to be rare, were in fact more common and hence worth less.

There were a few insightful purchasers, though. These were the customers who reported going back to the shops a few days later and purchasing the same souvenir with the revised date. They knew that in light of the stampede the rarest thing of all would be the full set – a mug with the wrong date and a twin with the right one.

So what does this tell us about how to be more persuasive? If you run a business, you should provide information to your customers about what is genuinely rare and unique about your products and services. Pointing out the features your product has that a competitor's doesn't can be a powerful route to getting them to say yes to your offering and not that of your competition. Similarly, colleagues at work might be persuaded to help you out on a project or initiative if they are told of its uniqueness: 'It's not often we get the chance to be involved in an initiative such as this.' Even family members are more likely to respond when told that your time and assistance are rare and dwindling. By simply and honestly pointing out the fact that your products, services, time and help are limited, you place a greater value on them to the point where people appreciate them and you more. And, in general, we say yes more to those we appreciate.

Quite a bit of scientific research supports the power of scarcity to influence our decision-making. We can also see the scarcity principle operating in everyday life. In recent years, even the 'holiday spirit' has become scarce, with parents practically fighting one another in shops at Christmas for nearly-out-of-stock gaming consoles. And in the UK, the petrol shortage in the summer of 2000 resulted in some extraordinary behaviour, as people scrambled to acquire the fuel that was so limited in availability. In another example, immediately after British Airways announced in February 2003 that it would be permanently grounding Concorde, the sale of seats on the plane did the opposite: they took off. And in October 2003 the notion of losing something caused many thousands of people to stop their cars and block a major motorway just to see Concorde's final take-off, a sight, it should be pointed out, that had been visible every single day for the previous thirty years or so.

We've all experienced the psychological effects of the scarcity principle in our daily lives. There is, however, a less tangible domain in which the principle operates both subtly and powerfully: the domain of information. Studies have demonstrated that information that is exclusive is viewed as both more valuable and more persuasive. For example, in a study conducted by researcher Amram Knishinsky, wholesale beef buyers more than doubled their orders when they were informed that a shortage of Australian beef was likely owing to weather conditions there. This is a clear demonstration of the effect of scarcity of the goods themselves. In addition, however, when those purchasers were told that the information came from an exclusive source and was not generally available to the rest of the public (both pieces of scarcity information were true), they increased their orders by a remarkable 600 per cent!

These findings offer a clear insight and applications that will make your requests more persuasive, in turn leading more people to accept your requests. If you pass along information that is unique to you, but fail to point out its exclusivity, you could be losing an excellent opportunity to use an effective and ethical influence technique.

37

What can you gain from loss?

On 23 April 1985, the Coca-Cola Company made a decision that *Time* magazine later dubbed 'the marketing fiasco of the decade': in response to data that more people preferred Pepsi's sweeter taste, they decided to take their traditional formula for Coke off the market and replace it with a sweeter 'New Coke'. Many of us remember that day. In the words of one news report, 'The Coca-Cola Company failed to foresee the sheer frustration and fury its action would create. From Bangor to Burbank, from Detroit to Dallas, tens of thousands of Coke lovers rose up as one to revile the taste of the new Coke and demand their old Coke back.'

Perhaps the most extreme example of this combined outrage and yearning comes from the story of a retired Seattle investor named Gay Mullins, who became something of a national celebrity by establishing a society called Old Cola Drinkers of America. This was a widespread group of people who worked tirelessly to get the traditional formula back on the market by using any civil, judicial or legislative means available. For instance, Mullins set up a hot line on which citizens could vent their rage and register their feelings, which received over sixty thousand calls. He distributed anti-New Coke buttons and T-shirts by the thousand. And he even tried to bring a class-action lawsuit against the Coca-Cola Company, which was quickly dismissed by a federal judge. What's most astonishing about Mr Mullins's behaviour is that it didn't matter to him that in blind taste tests, he either preferred New Coke over the original or couldn't tell the difference between them.

Note that the thing Mr Mullins *liked more* was less valuable to him than the thing he felt he was *losing*. We'll come back to this idea in a moment. In the meantime, however, it's worth noting that even after giving in to customer demands and bringing the original Coke back to the shelves, company officials were stung and somewhat perplexed by what had hit them. As Donald Keough, then president of the Coca-Cola Company, said about consumers' diehard loyalty to the original Coke, 'It's a wonderful American mystery, a lovely American enigma. And you can't measure it any more than you can measure love, pride, or patriotism.'

We disagree. First off, it's no mystery if you understand the psychology of the scarcity principle, and particularly how it relates to people's sensitivities to losing something they already have. This is especially the case for a product that's as wrapped up in people's histories and traditions as Coca-Cola has always been throughout the world.

Second, this natural inclination on the part of Coca-Cola drinkers is not only something that *can* be measured, but something that we think the Coca-Cola Company *had* measured – in their own market research, no less. It was sitting right there in front of them before they made their infamous decision to change, but they hadn't combined their own data with an understanding of social influence factors.

The people of the Coca-Cola Company are no penny-pinchers when it comes to market research; they've been willing to spend millions of dollars to ensure that they've analysed the market correctly for new products. Before their decision to switch to the new Coke, from 1981 to 1984 they very carefully tested the new and old formulas on nearly 200,000 people in 25 cities. What they found in their taste tests, most of which were blind, was a clear preference, 55 per cent to 45 per cent, for the *new* Coke over the old. Some of the tests, however, were not conducted with unmarked samples. In these ones, the participants were told which was the old and which was the new Coke beforehand. Under those conditions, the preference for the new Coke *increased* by an additional 6 per cent.

How does that fit with the fact that people expressed a clear preference for the *old* Coke when the company finally introduced the new Coke? The only way it can be made to fit is by applying the principle of scarcity to the puzzle: during the taste tests, it was the new Coke which was unavailable to people to buy, and so, when they knew which sample was which, they showed an especially strong preference for what they couldn't otherwise have. But later, when the company replaced the traditional recipe with the new one, now it was the old Coke that people couldn't have and *it* became the favourite.

So, a 6 per cent increase in preference for the new Coke was right there in the company's research when they looked at the difference between blind and identified taste test results. The problem is that they simply interpreted it incorrectly. They probably said to themselves, 'Oh, good, this means that when people know that they're getting something new, their desire for it will shoot up.' But in fact what that 6 per cent increase really meant was that when people know what it is they *can't have*, their desire for it will shoot up.

Even more powerfully than simply making a product unavailable, removing the original Coke from the shelves meant that lifetime Coke drinkers were actually losing something they used to have on a regular basis. And the tendency to be more sensitive to possible losses than to possible gains is one of the best-supported findings in social science. Behavioural researchers Daniel Kahneman and Amos Tversky were the first to test and document the notion of 'loss aversion'. This can explain quite a bit of human behaviour, in areas including finance, decision-making, negotiation and persuasion.

For example, one consequence of loss aversion is that it often motivates inexperienced investors to prematurely sell stocks that have gained in value because they don't want to lose what they've already gained. Similarly, the desire to avoid any potential for a loss also motivates these investors to hold on to stocks that have lost value since the date of purchase. Because selling the stock at that point would be to formally and irrevocably take a loss on the investment, many of these investors are reluctant to do so, a decision that often results in further stock price decline.

Loss aversion is also important from a marketing standpoint. Generally speaking, marketers and advertisers are focused on getting across the message about the benefits of their product to potential customers. In attempting to do so, they often frame their message in terms of what the prospective clients have to gain from the product. In such cases, however, they may well be wasting an opportunity to present their message in an entirely more persuasive way by focusing on what the audience stands to lose. Rather than using language such as 'Take this opportunity to try our new product line at a 20 per cent discount', they might be more successful using language such as 'Don't miss out on this opportunity to try our new product line at a 20 per cent discount'. In the latter example, they would be pointing out to the audience that because the deal is scarce in some way (e.g. available for a limited time), they're in danger of losing the opportunity to purchase the products with the current discount.

Similarly, if you're hoping to persuade your colleagues to work with you on a particular project, it's important to point out not just what they stand to gain in terms of opportunities and experience but also that they stand to lose out on those factors. In fact, research conducted by social scientist Marjorie Shelley has shown that potential losses figure far more heavily in managers' decision-making than the same things presented as gains. For example, let's say you have an idea that, if adopted, will potentially produce savings of up to £100,000 a year for your department. Instead of presenting that idea as a saving, you're likely to be more persuasive if you frame the initiative in terms of losing the same amount if it fails to get adopted.

The notion of loss is compelling in terms of the messages that we receive too. When posing as representatives from a local utilities company, researchers from the University of California found that one group of homeowners were up to 300 per cent more likely to carry out recommended energy efficiency improvements in their home when they were told that they would continue to lose an average of 50 cents a day than home-owners who were told they could save 50 cents a day. Notice that in this example there is no economic difference in the message. The 50 cents remain the same economically, but psychologically the loss-framed message generated a threefold increase in persuasion.

It's also crucial to remember that you can be unduly influenced by this strategy. For example, some devious negotiators – or even car salespeople – will wait until just before a final agreement appears to be within reach to throw in an unpalatable, take-it-or-leave-it demand, knowing full well that their counterparts are going to be disinclined to walk away; after all, walking away would mean a lot of lost time, effort and opportunity (also known as 'sunk costs'). If you believe a salesperson with whom you're negotiating is manipulating your loss aversion in this way, you should make sure that it's the salesperson who feels the loss.

38

Which single word will strengthen your persuasion attempts?

Based on L. Frank Baum's famous children's storybook, the 1939 film *The Wizard of Oz* remains today a traditional family favourite. Many of us are familiar with the plight of Dorothy and her friends the Scarecrow, the Tin Man and the Lion as they make their perilous journey along the Yellow Brick Road. Clearly, the Wizard of Oz had succeeded in persuading them that he was both benevolent and powerful. But what can the tune the four travellers sang along the way – 'Because because because because! / Of all the wonderful things he does' – tell us about how we can successfully persuade others to follow the paths we lay out for them?

Let's think about queuing. Whether you're at a bank, a supermarket or an amusement park, queuing is probably not your idea of fun. Considering the almost universal motivation to get through the line as quickly as possible, under what circumstances would you be willing to let another person cut in front of you? A central theme to this book is that small changes in the way that requests are made can often lead to startlingly big results. But is it possible that just a single word from a requester could drastically increase the likelihood that you'd say 'yes, go ahead'?

Yes – and the word is *because*. Behavioural scientist Ellen

Langer and her colleagues decided to put the persuasive power of this word to the test. In one study, Langer arranged for a stranger to approach someone waiting in line to use a photocopier and simply ask, 'Excuse me, I have five pages. May I use the Xerox machine?' Faced with this direct request to cut ahead in the line, 60 per cent of the people agreed to allow the stranger to go ahead of them. When the stranger followed the request with a reason, however ('May I use the Xerox machine, because I'm in a rush?'), almost everyone (94 per cent) complied. This kind of boost may not seem very surprising. After all, providing a solid reason for the request justifies asking to jump ahead.

Here's where the study gets really interesting: Langer tested one more version of the request. This time, the stranger also used the word *because*, but followed it with a completely meaningless reason. Specifically, the stranger said, 'May I use the Xerox machine, because I have to make copies?' Because you have to *make copies*? Of course you want to use the photocopier to make copies – you're not going to use it to sharpen your pencil, are you? Despite the tautological hollowness of the 'reason' the stranger provided, it generated nearly the same elevated levels of compliance as when the reason was wholly legitimate (93 per cent).

The Xerox study demonstrates the unique motivational influence of the word *because*. The word gets its persuasive power from the continually reinforced association over the course of our lives between *because* and the good rationales that typically follow it (e.g. '... because it would help me get that promotion', '... because I'm running out of time', '... because England's national team has some of the best strikers in the world').

Of course, like most things, the power of *because* has its limits. In the Xerox study, compliance was equally high no matter how poor the rationale that followed *because*. But in those cases, the request was small – the requester only asked to make five copies. To see what would happen with a larger favour, Langer introduced another set of experimental conditions. The requester told this group of participants that she needed to make twenty copies. Anyone who has ever used a copy machine knows that the chances that the machine will jam seem to rise exponentially with each added page. In other words, participants' answers to this larger request may have a substantially greater impact on them than their answer to a request that involves less.

This time, when the stranger simply made her request without using the word *because*, only 24 per cent complied. But how about those who gave a bad reason – those who said, '... because I need to make copies?' This produced no increase in compliance at all. When the larger request was made with a good reason, however ('... because I'm in a hurry'), the response rate doubled. Taken together, the results of this study suggest that when the stakes are low, people are more likely to take mental short cuts when deciding how to behave, rather than thinking hard about the issue. On the other hand, when the stakes are high, people really do take the strength of the requester's reasoning into consideration when deciding how to respond.

These findings serve as a reminder to always be sure to accompany your requests with a strong rationale, even when you think the reasons might be fairly clear. For example, when booking a meeting with a customer or when asking a co-worker to cooperate on a new project, be sure to state the reasoning behind your request. That may sound obvious, but too often we mistakenly assume that other people understand the reasons behind our requests.

This strategy is also likely to pay dividends at home. Rather than demanding that your children 'come to the table for dinner now' or 'go to bed immediately', a more effective strategy would be to provide a reason why you are asking them to take that action – and not just '*because* I said so!'

It's important to note that the word *because* works both ways. You should try to get other people to say *because* to you. For instance, suppose that you work for an IT firm. Your long-term customers may have got used to working with your company, but with each passing year the reasons for sticking with your company may have become less salient, or, even worse, entirely forgotten. Consequently, your business can be left vulnerable to competitors. One effective way to strengthen your business ties and your clients' confidence in your company is to have the decision-makers at your client's firm generate reasons for why they use your business. This could be accomplished through feedback surveys, in which the clients are asked to describe why they like doing business with your company. Research by Gregory Maio and colleagues suggests that this procedure will strengthen your clients' commitment to your firm by reminding them that the continued relationship is rational rather than simply habitual. In other words, get people to say *because* to you, and like Dorothy and her travel companions, they'll end up singing your praises, too.

39

When might asking for all the reasons be a mistake?

'First, do no harm'. Although the Hippocratic oath applies first and foremost to medical practitioners' obligations to their patients, it surely holds for advertisers' obligations towards the products they are trying to sell. At the very least, they shouldn't *hurt* sales of the goods and services they're trying to sell. But how might a well-intentioned copywriter actually drive potential consumers towards a competitor?

Recall from the previous chapter that having people generate reasons why they're in favour of a certain position can be a highly effective strategy for strengthening their beliefs in that position. If we apply this thinking to advertisements, it seems wise to encourage consumers to think of as many reasons as possible to choose our goods and services. Recent research suggests, however, that under certain circumstances this strategy can actually backfire.

Imagine you're in the market for a new premium automobile, and you've narrowed your choices down to either a BMW or a Mercedes. You open a magazine and see an ad for BMW that says the following: 'BMW or Mercedes? There are many reasons to choose a BMW. Can you name ten?'

In one study conducted by Michaela Wänke and her colleagues, a group of business students saw an ad just like this among several other advertisements. A different group of business students at the same university saw a slightly different ad – one that stated, 'BMW or Mercedes? There are many reasons to choose a BMW. Can you name *one*?' (emphasis added).

Afterwards, the participants were asked for their opinions about BMW and Mercedes, including their interest in one day purchasing a vehicle from either of those brands. The results were clear: the advertising copy that asked readers to name ten reasons to choose a BMW led to *lower* evaluations of the BMW and higher evaluations of Mercedes than the copy that asked the readers to name just one reason to choose a BMW.

What's responsible for this backfire effect? The researchers explain that participants in this study based their judgements of BMW on how easy they found it to come up with reasons in support of this brand. When they were asked to name only one reason, participants had a relatively easy time. Faced with naming ten, however, the task was hard. So, rather than using the *number* of reasons they generated as the best indicator for their evaluations, the participants instead based their judgements on the *ease or difficulty* of the process of generating reasons. More generally, psychologists refer to the ease or difficulty of experiencing something as the 'fluency' of that experience, a concept we'll be coming back to.

The data from this study indicate that before asking your audience to generate multiple reasons in support of your position, it's important to consider just how easily they'll be able to do so. If the task seems like a relatively difficult one, ask them instead to generate just a few reasons. The findings also suggest a rather ironic strategy: you can potentially give yourself a competitive edge by asking your audience to generate a large number of reasons *in favour of your rival's offerings*. The harder it is for the audience to come up with a large number of rationales, the better your goods, services or initiatives will look in comparison.

Other research has shown that the ease or difficulty of merely *imagining* using a product will also affect consumers' decisions. Research conducted by social scientist Petia Petrova has demonstrated that encouraging customers to imagine themselves experiencing the delights of a restaurant or holiday destination only increases the desire to visit if it's easy to imagine doing so.

Along these lines, you might want to consider the extent to which your product, or more generally your request for the behaviour you'd like your audience to undertake, involves actions that are novel or foreign to them. For instance, you may want to persuade a consumer group to purchase a brand-new product marketed by your company. If this product has complicated technical features with which the group has little or no experience and which have not yet been fully explained, it may be difficult for your prospects to imagine themselves actually using the product, which will make them less likely to select it.

Another arena where these findings are clearly important is in advertising production. Art directors are often given free rein to generate images that are eye-catching or memorable, but in the process they may create pictures that are abstract, giving little consideration to how their images affect the target audience's ability to visualise themselves using the product. This research shows that concrete images are likely to be more effective than abstract ones. In addition, the decision-making process in these types of cases can be improved through greater collaboration with the copywriters, prior testing of the ads, and focus groups that are specifically geared towards understanding how easy or difficult it is for a relevant audience to imagine themselves in the relevant situations.

40

How can the simplicity of a name make it appear more valuable?

When he was once asked the complex question of what the stock market would do next, J. P. Morgan reportedly gave a simple response: 'It will fluctuate.' But how can the power of simplicity – particularly in the naming of your product, project or even your company – help you boost your influence?

According to social scientists Adam Alter and Daniel Oppenheimer, people tend to have a greater affection for words and names that are easy to pronounce – words or names that have a high degree of fluency – than for those that are hard to pronounce. They argue that people feel more positively towards company names and stock symbols that are easier to read and to pronounce than those with more difficult names. One consequence of this psychological tendency is that the easier a company name or stock symbol is to read or pronounce, the more valuable it should seem, leading the stock prices to increase.

To first test this hypothesis in a controlled study, they generated the names of fictitious stocks that were either fluent or disfluent. They told participants that these were real companies and asked them to estimate the future performance of each of the stocks. The results were clear: not only did participants predict that the pronounceable stocks (e.g. Slingerman, Vander,

Tanley) would outperform the others (e.g. Sagxter, Frurio, Xagibdan), they also predicted that the former would rise in value, whereas the latter would fall.

To find out whether this happened in the real world, Alter and Oppenheimer randomly picked 89 companies whose shares were traded on the New York Stock Exchange and had their initial public offering between 1990 and 2004. They then looked at the relationship between the fluency of a stock name and its performance one day, one week, six months and one year after its initial public offering. The researchers found that if a person had invested $1,000 in the ten most fluently named companies on the list the investment would have outperformed its counterpart in the group of ten least fluently named companies for each of the designated time periods, including a $333 difference just one year after the initial public offering. What's more, in a separate study the authors separated over 750 companies listed on the New York Stock Exchange or the American Stock Exchange by whether or not their stock ticker symbol was pronounceable (e.g. KAR) or unpronounceable (e.g. RDO), and found similar results.

So, are we recommending that you go right out and trade in your shares of Mxyzptlk Holding Corp. in exchange for Yahoo! stock, fire your financial adviser or have a garage sale to rid yourself of your stock-picking monkeys and dartboards? Not quite. We are, however, advising you not to underestimate the power of simplicity, even in the name you give your company, product or initiative. Often, people are so focused on seemingly more influential aspects of their projects that they overlook the first piece of information that will be communicated to its audience – its name. All else being equal, the easier it is to read and pronounce, the more likely consumers, potential stockholders or other decision-makers will be to view it positively.

In a similar vein, researchers have found that the persuasiveness of a handwritten message is influenced by the quality of the handwriting: the worse the handwriting, the less persuasive the message will be. As with the processes described in the last two chapters, this is the case because readers will mistakenly interpret the sense of difficulty they feel when they read a message with bad handwriting as a sense of difficulty in believing the content of the message. At least on the surface of things, there appears to be an easy and accessible solution for those of us who are calligraphically challenged: can't we just type out our persuasive messages? Yes, but even that advice comes with a caveat: research has demonstrated that your arguments are likely to be deemed far more persuasive if they are in an easy-to-read font.

The findings of all this research also have more general implications for how people choose to communicate with one another. Take, for example, the fact that communicators frequently try to convey their erudition via their grandiloquent, magniloquent, sesquipedalian verbosity; in other words, they try to look smart by using unnecessarily long words or overly technical jargon.* Consider, for instance, the following communication sent out by a manager to his team, as reported in the *New York Post* in October 2006: 'We're leveraging our assets and establishing strategic alliances to create a robust knowledge center – one with a customer-ruled business structure using market-leading technologies to maximize our human systems.'

Huh? This apparently means 'We're consultants'. Recent research has shown that using overly complex language like this can produce the exact opposite of the intended effect: because the audience has difficulty interpreting the language, the

---

* Something we, of course, would never do.

message is deemed less convincing and the author is perceived to be less intelligent.

Regrettably, these kinds of messages are all too frequent in everyday life, whether in business communications, healthcare advice or students' essays. For example, a poll taken at Stanford University found that 86.4 per cent of the students surveyed admitted they had used complicated language in their academic essays to try to make themselves sound smarter. More disturbing, however, is the finding from a UK-based consulting firm that 56 per cent of employees thought that their managers and supervisors didn't communicate clearly with them and often used incomprehensible language that confused the messages. One way to avoid these problems is to share these messages with, and get feedback from, colleagues not directly connected to the project prior to sending the messages out.

41

How can rhyme make your influence climb?

'From Michigan State direct to your plate'. Which company made this statement, and what was it referring to? It was a slogan used by the Heinz Corporation to advertise their baked beans. Founded in 1869 by Henry John Heinz in Sharpsburg, Pennsylvania, the company started out as a supplier of condiments to local grocers, first delivering horseradish, then pickles and then tomato ketchup by horse-drawn carriage. In 1896, Heinz noticed an advertisement for '21 styles of shoes'. He decided that his own products were not styles, but varieties, and although he had more than sixty foods in production at that point, he adopted the slogan '57 Varieties' because he favoured the numbers 5 and 7. Thus, a new advertising campaign was launched. The Heinz 57 Varieties slogan is still used today, along with a number of other notable Heinz advertisements, including the rhyming ad for their baked beans.

Launched in the 1960s, a typical British version of this television commercial would depict a mother preparing supper for her two children, who arrive home unexpectedly with a group of their hungry friends, only to plead something like, 'Mum, can Sally and Robin and Jeffrey and Debbie stay for tea please?' After a brief, exasperated look, the welcoming mum would go to the cupboard and take out more tins of Heinz baked beans.

The jingle would then begin: 'A million housewives every day pick up a tin of beans and say Beanz Meanz Heinz'.

The impact of these advertisements was considered so great that the Heinz Corporation continued to run them for more than three decades. In fact, at the time the ads were shown in the UK, a significant number of people, if stopped randomly in the street and asked to finish the line 'a million housewives every day pick up a tin of beans and say ...', would, without hesitation, say, 'Beanz Meanz Heinz.'

What is particularly fascinating about one of the more famous of the Heinz advertisements is that it didn't set out to inform the consumer of any particular attributes or benefits of the product. It merely put the product name into a rhyme. Out of all the potential advertisement strategies to choose from, why would Heinz create a message that rhymed? Part of it may be that ads that rhyme are more likeable, memorable and easily repeated to others. But could it be that rhyming statements are also seen as more accurate and truthful?

Noting the pervasiveness of rhyming proverbs such as 'Birds of a feather flock together', social scientists Matthew McGlone and Jessica Tofighbakhsh set out to investigate whether statements that rhyme are seen as more accurate than those that don't. As part of their study, they took a number of rhyming sayings previously unknown to the participants and created parallel but non-rhyming versions of them. For example, they took the relatively obscure saying 'Caution and measure will win you treasure' and modified it to say, 'Caution and measure will win you riches'. As another example, they took the saying 'What sobriety conceals, alcohol reveals' and changed it to 'What sobriety conceals, alcohol unmasks'.

Participants then read some of these sayings and rated each one for the extent to which it reflected the way the world really works. The researchers found that even though all the participants strongly held the belief that rhyming was in no way an indicator of accuracy, they nonetheless perceived the statements that rhymed as more accurate than those that didn't.

The researchers explained that rhyming phrases are characterised by greater processing fluency, meaning that they're mentally processed more easily than non-rhyming phrases. Because people tend to base accuracy evaluations, at least partly, on the perceived fluency of the incoming information, the rhyming statements are judged as more accurate.

These findings have many applications in everyday life. For one, they suggest that when marketers and business operators think about what slogans, mottos, trademarks and jingles to employ, they would be well advised to consider that using rhymes should increase not only the likeability of the message, but its perceived truthfulness as well. Perhaps this is why, when asked what a company could say about their product when there was nothing new to say, a seasoned advertising executive replied, 'Well, if you have nothing to say about your product, then I suppose you can always sing about it.'

Second, parents might be advised to use rhyme to their advantage when faced with a common and frustrating challenge – getting their kids to go to bed. After you've enjoyed some quality time reading nursery rhymes with them, perhaps getting them to join in a few verses of 'It's off to bed for sleepy head' will prove persuasive.

Finally, the power of rhyme can even be applied in a legal setting. In fact, the authors of this research point out one infamous rhyme that seems so weighty that it just may have tipped the scales of justice. During O. J. Simpson's murder trial, Johnnie Cochran, Simpson's defence attorney, told the jury, 'If the gloves don't fit, you must acquit!' Considering the subtle influence of rhyme, the study's authors may be right to question how the verdict might have been affected if Cochran had instead implored, 'If the gloves don't fit, you must find him not guilty!'

42 What can batting practice tell us about persuasion?

Sports can be a useful training ground for those of us who wish to become more persuasive. At a baseball game, for example, it's relatively common to see players place a weighted ring around their bat before they take their warm-up swings. According to the ballplayers, repeatedly swinging a heavier bat makes the unweighted bat feel lighter in comparison.

The principle underlying this effect is known in the social sciences as perceptual contrast. Simply put, the characteristics of objects are perceived not in a vacuum, but in comparison with others. For example, if you are asked to pick up a 10kg weight in a gymnasium, it will appear lighter if you had first picked up a 20kg weight and heavier if you had first picked up a 5kg weight. Nothing has changed about the 10kg weight – except your perception of it. This psychological process is not limited to weight; it holds for almost any type of judgement you could make. In every case the pattern is the same: what you experience first determines the perception of the next thing you experience.

Social psychologists Zakary Tormala and Richard Petty recently applied these principles to show how contrast effects can influence persuasion. Specifically, they looked at how the *amount of information* people think they have about something can be influenced by the amount they learn about something else. These researchers asked people to read a persuasive message for a fictitious department store called Brown's (the 'target message'), but only after reading a persuasive message for a different fictitious department store called Smith's ('the prior message'). The target message was the same for all participants in the experiment – it described three departments of Brown's. The researchers altered, however, the amount of information the prior message contained about Smith's, from a comparatively small amount (one department) to a large amount (six departments). They found that when the prior message contained a great deal of information, the target message was seen as less persuasive and produced less favourable attitudes towards the department store, whereas the opposite occurred when the prior message contained very little information. It seems that the participants felt more knowledgeable about Brown's after learning relatively little about Smith's, and vice versa. This is the perceptual contrast effect in action.

To extend their findings, the researchers conducted a similar study; the only difference was that, prior to receiving persuasive information about Brown's department store, participants received a little or a lot of persuasive information about a car (the Mini Cooper). The results were consistent with the earlier study, suggesting that the prior information doesn't even need to be all that relevant to affect the persuasive impact of a subsequent message.

This idea can be applied to sales. Imagine that your company sells a line of products, and you're confident that one particular product would provide the best fit for your prospective client. You should be sure to discuss its merits at length after you've spent a much shorter period of time discussing another product. This idea, as we have already seen when it comes to wine, applies to prices, too.

What's interesting to note is that perceptual contrast offers us a very efficient means of persuasion. Often we don't have the luxury of changing our products, services or requests – it would be far too costly and time-consuming. But we can change what our products, services and requests are compared with. To give just one real-world example, a home improvement company was able to increase the sales of one of its top-of-the-range backyard hot tubs by over 500 per cent simply by (a) telling prospective customers, honestly, that many buyers of the top-of-the-range model reported that having it was like adding an extra room to the house and then (b) asking them to consider how much it would cost to build another room on to the side of their house. After all, a £7,000 spa seems much less expensive when compared with construction that would cost at least twice as much.

43

How can you gain a head start in the quest for loyalty?

Whether it's free cups of coffee, money-off vouchers, discounted flights or coupons towards your next holiday, many companies try to increase customer loyalty by offering incentives. The results of some recent research offer insights into how you can increase the likelihood that others will be more loyal to you and more interested in what you have to offer.

Consumer researchers Joseph Nunes and Xavier Dreze thought that customers involved in incentive programmes would show more loyalty towards the company and reach the pay-off milestones more quickly if the company gave them a head start – even without decreasing the number of purchases needed to reach the reward.

In one study, loyalty cards were handed out to 300 customers of a local car wash. The customers were told that every time they bought a car wash, their loyalty card would be stamped. There were, however, two types of card. One type stated that eight stamps were required to receive a free car wash, and no stamps were attached to the card. The other kind stated that ten stamps were required to receive the free wash, but two stamps were already affixed. This meant that both cards required eight purchases to receive the award, but the second group seemed well on its way.

Subsequently, every time a customer came back for another wash, an employee affixed a stamp to the card and wrote down the date of purchase. After several months, when the researchers ended the programme and looked at the data, their hypotheses had been confirmed: whereas only 19 per cent of customers in the eight-stamp group made enough visits to claim their free car wash, 34 per cent of the ten-stamp, head-start group did so. What's more, the head-start group took less time to complete their eighth purchase, taking an average of 2.9 fewer days between visits to the car wash.

According to Nunes and Dreze, reframing the programme as one that's been started but is incomplete rather than one that has not yet begun means that people feel more motivated to complete it. They also pointed to research showing that the closer people get towards completing a goal, the more effort they exert to achieve it. In support of this idea, the data revealed that the amount of time between visits decreased by about half a day on average with every additional car wash.

Besides the obvious application of these findings to loyalty programmes of all sorts, the results of this study suggest that when soliciting another person for help with anything, you should try to point out how that person has already taken steps towards the completion of that task. For example, if you need help with a project that's similar to one that this person has worked on in the past, you could emphasise how, in essence, she is well on her way to overcoming the complexities involved in finishing it. And if that's not the case, but you've already done a fair amount of work on the project, you could underscore how the task is already almost 30 per cent completed.

As another example, suppose you are a sales manager. Your sales team has a target, but the team isn't doing too well in the early stages. If you learned that a large sale that will be processed centrally is already in the offing, rather than keeping the information to yourself, thinking that you might use it to fall back on if your team doesn't hit the target, you should consider publicising it. In this way, you'd present an effect of progression towards the goal.

Teachers and parents can also benefit from such a strategy. Imagine that your child is being particularly stubborn about doing his homework and you feel compelled to offer incentives. If you decided to give him one weekend off from homework for every six weekends on which he does it, you might find that he would be especially motivated to comply if you started him off with 'credit' for one weekend before your programme officially begins.

The message is clear: people will be more likely to stick with programmes and tasks if you can offer them some evidence of how they've already made progress towards completing them. If you use this strategy, like cars at a car wash, your influence will sparkle.

44

What can a box of crayons teach us about persuasion?

Gone are the days when the names of colours were simple. Anyone who opens a new box of crayons will quickly notice that the old common names (e.g. green, yellow, brown) have been replaced by names such as Tropical Rainforest, Laser Lemon and Fuzzy-wuzzy Brown. How can a colour name like Cornflower or Razzmatazz help you keep your company's chips blue and your business out of the red?

Researchers Elizabeth Miller and Barbara Kahn noticed this aspect about crayons and countless other products, and sought to better understand how these kinds of differences in names influence consumer preferences. As part of their research they distinguished between four categories of colour and flavour names:

(1) common, which are typical and unspecific (e.g. blue);

(2) common descriptive, which are typical and specific (e.g. sky blue);

(3) unexpected descriptive, which are atypical and specific (e.g. Kermit green); and

(4) ambiguous, which are atypical and unspecific (e.g. millennium orange).

The researchers suggest that unexpected descriptive (3) and ambiguous (4) colour and flavour names should elicit more positive feelings towards a given product than the other two types (1 and 2) of colour and flavour names. These two types of names are, however, effective for different reasons. Unexpected descriptive names, such as Kermit green, are effective because they act as a sort of puzzle to be solved, which typically leads people to consider more aspects of the products – particularly the positive ones. Although solving this little puzzle may not qualify consumers to join Mensa, it may create an 'aha!' moment that could lead them to associate positive emotions with the product. Ambiguous names, such as millennium orange, prompt consumers to try to discover, in the absence of any meaningful information, what the makers of the product are trying to convey with that name. This also leads consumers to think about the positive aspects the company is trying to highlight with the name. Miller and Kahn confirmed their hypotheses using a variety of names for jelly bean flavours and for sweater colours.

What are the implications for businesses? One answer would be that businesses should not shy away from using less-than-straightforward names for certain aspects of its products.* But this approach doesn't just work for products and services. Let's say, for example, that you're looking to gain resources from colleagues at work to support a new project or training initiative. By using what might be considered to be an unexpected title or name for the project, or even an ambiguous one, you might well foster a sense of fascination and attraction to it.

We can also put the lessons of this research into practice at

---

* Note that these less-than-straightforward names should still be easily readable and pronounceable, as we discussed in Chapter 40.

home. For instance, when our kids are considering whether to go out for dinner with their friends or eat at home, jazzing up the label we give to the dish (e.g. 'chicken surprise' instead of plain old 'chicken') may convince them to stay at home for the night. Of course, when we'd rather have a quiet night at home, coming up instead with 'broccoli and Brussels sprouts' is always an option ...

45

How can you package your message to ensure it keeps going, and going, and going?

Who am I? I'm pink. I'm a toy rabbit. I have a drum. And I'm powered by a brand-name battery that outlasts the competition. Who am I?

Depending on where you live, I'm either the Energizer Bunny or the Duracell Bunny. Confused? You're not alone.

To clarify things, and to better understand what this confusion can tell us about effective persuasion and marketing, a little history lesson is in order. The very first pink, battery-powered bunny with a penchant for persistent percussion on television was the Duracell Bunny. To be more accurate, it wasn't a single toy rabbit, but rather a whole species – the Duracell Bunnies – whose power was said to be longer-lasting than that from any other brand of batteries. In one ad, for instance, a number of drum-beating toy rabbits, each powered by a different brand of battery, slowly come to a standstill, leaving only one – powered by Duracell – still full of energy.

Over fifteen years ago, however, Duracell failed to renew its trademark in the United States, which allowed its competitor, Energizer, to swoop in and trademark its own pink, alkaline-powered drumming bunny in an effort to mock the Duracell campaign and claim its products' superiority. This is why, these days, North American television viewers are accustomed to seeing their bunnies running on Energizer, whereas it's Duracell for those in the rest of the world.

In the Energizer television commercials, viewers think they are watching an advertisement for another product (e.g. Sit-again Haemorrhoid Ointment), which is interrupted by the Energizer walking through the frame to the narration of '… still going, and going, and going, and going … nothing outlasts the Energizer'. Despite the early public and critical acclaim that these ads received for the Energizer Bunny's off-the-wall and into-other-advertisement antics, there was just one problem: many people, even those who loved the ads, couldn't remember which company's batteries were being advertised. In fact, one survey showed that, even among viewers who chose the bunny ads as their favourite ads of the year, an astonishing 40 per cent were certain that the ads were for Duracell. This was the case even though there are plenty of features that distinguish the Energizer Bunny from its copper-top counterpart, including bigger ears, sunglasses, a larger drum and fur that's a brighter shade of pink. And, not to be forgotten, whereas the Duracell Bunnies have to walk around non-stop on their bare feet, the bulkier Energizer Bunny gets to wear flip-flops.

Confusion between the two company's bunnies certainly played a role here. But, as it turns out, even many people who'd never seen the Duracell ads misremembered which brand sponsored these newer commercials, thinking it was Duracell. In fact, shortly after the ads became popular, it was *Duracell's* market share which grew, while Energizer's shrunk a bit.

What action should Energizer have taken to prevent such a problem, and what lessons can we learn from it? The psychological research is clear: placing a memory aid on store displays and on the actual packaging of their product – for example, an image of the Energizer Bunny with the text 'Keeps going and going and going ...' – would have done much to correct consumers' faulty memories as well as product choices that they based on those memories. And that's exactly what the company eventually did, with great success.

What's the implication for advertising in general? Increasingly, companies try to brand themselves via extensive media campaigns that emphasise the key element of their brand (e.g. durability or quality or economy) through a character that epitomises it. They assume that viewers will connect their products with the branded element while exposed to the ads, which is a reasonable assumption provided that the ads are properly constructed. They also assume that viewers will recall the connection when ready to buy – and that's naive. Consumers' memories, subjected to hundreds of thousands of these associations in the course of modern life, aren't up to the task – at least not without the assistance of point-of-purchase cues that revive the desired connection. It's for this reason that any major advertising campaign needs to integrate the essential images, characters or slogans of the ads into the in-store product displays and product packaging the consumer sees when making a purchase decision. Although changing the display and packaging to match the central features of the media campaign may be more expensive in the short term, it's essential.

This strategy isn't limited to marketing products; it can also be used to market information and ideas. Consider, for example, the massive challenge you'd face if you were part of a health organisation devoted to reducing alcohol abuse on university campuses. Even if you were capable of creating an advertising campaign that motivated students, when they read the message to drink less, how would you ensure that it stayed in their minds when it's most necessary?

To take an example, one type of persuasion campaign that's

become increasingly popular with university health administrators who are trying to battle student alcohol abuse has been dubbed 'social norms marketing'. Researchers have found that students typically overestimate the number of drinks that their peers consume; and, as we know from our discussions of social proof, people tend to behave in line with perceived social norms. The goal of social norms marketing campaigns is to reduce the frequency of college student alcohol abuse by correcting students' misperceptions. For example, a social norms marketing poster might state that a survey shows that '65 per cent of students at our university have 3 or fewer drinks when they party'. The thinking is that providing the sign's readers with more accurate figures for the amount that their peers drink will reduce the amount that they'll want to drink when they party.

Although these programmes show signs of promise, the current evidence for their success is mixed. Even though these posters may be quite persuasive when students actually read them, perhaps one of the reasons why the campaigns are not more effective is that when they get into drinking situations, students either forget about or aren't focused on that information. For instance, posters, signs and other forms of media conveying anti-alcohol messages in normative campaigns are commonly (and understandably, from a practical point of view) placed in libraries, classrooms, student unions, health centres and in common areas of residence halls rather than in the settings where drinking is most likely to occur. Unfortunately, the lack of connection between where students see the information and where they are when they drink means that the distant voice of the message is likely to be drowned out by the here-and-now sounds of clanking bottles and drunken laughter prevalent in bars, clubs, parties and halls of residence.

The memory aid research indicates that the likelihood of students focusing on the social norms information in the appropriate settings could be strengthened by placing the campaign's logo on objects native to those settings (e.g. coasters, entrance bracelets, hand stamps). Alternatively, the campus could give away items that have the campaign's logo imprinted on them, such as frisbees. Students would then be likely to take them back to their lodgings or halls of residence, where they would be more likely to see the memory aid. (Ironically, this strategy might even be more effective once the students get some alcohol in them, as some research shows that simple persuasive messages tend to be more successful when people are drinking.) Similarly, some communities have tried to fight drink-driving by getting participating bar owners to put into patrons' drinks something called 'light cubes', which are LED lights enclosed in plastic in the shape of ice cubes. Emitting flashes of red and blue light, these memory aids typically have the effect of making the drink look like police car lights, serving as a persuasive extension of the long arm of the law.

All in all, regardless of whether they are for public or private campaigns, memory aids will ensure that your message doesn't fade, but keeps on going, and going, and going ...

46

What object can persuade people to reflect on their values?

Mirror, mirror, on the wall, what's one of the most persuasive objects of them all? Actually, mirror, you are.

No one doubts that the primary purpose of a mirror is to see what we look like on the outside, but mirrors also act as windows into what we look like – and, perhaps more important, what we *want* to look like – on the inside. As a result, viewing ourselves in a mirror causes us to act in more socially desirable ways.

Take, for example, a study conducted by social scientist Arthur Beaman and his colleagues on Halloween. Rather than conducting the study in a university laboratory or on the street, Beaman temporarily converted eighteen local houses into makeshift research facilities. When trick-or-treaters rang the doorbell of one of the houses used, a research assistant greeted them, asked them their names and then pointed to a large bowl of confectionery sitting on a nearby table. After telling the children that they could each take *one* of the sweets, she mentioned that she had some work to do, and quickly left the room. That was the treat part of the experiment. And here's the trick: what the children didn't know, besides the fact that they were in a cleverly devised experiment, was that someone was watching them through a hidden peephole. That person was another research assistant who had the job of recording whether each child behaved dishonestly by taking more than one sweet.

When the results were in, the data revealed that over a third of the kids took more than they should have – 33.7 per cent, to be exact. But the researchers wanted to see whether they could reduce the rate of confectionery theft through the use of a mirror. In these cases, before the bell rang, the research assistant angled a large mirror by the confectionery bowl in such a way that the trick-or-treaters had to look at themselves in the mirror when they took the sweets. The theft rate with the mirror? Only 8.9 per cent.

In a similar vein, one of us conducted a study examining how focusing people on themselves and their own image makes them act more consistently with their values. Led by behavioural scientist Carl Kallgren, we first assessed participants' feelings about littering at the beginning of an academic term. Later in the term, when participants arrived at the laboratory, half were exposed to a closed-circuit television featuring their own image (so that it was almost like seeing themselves in a mirror), while the other half watched a closed-circuit television featuring geometric shapes. They were told that they would be completing a task that required their heart rate to be monitored, which involved placing some gel on their hand. Once the subjects believed that their part in the study was over, a research assistant handed them a paper towel to wipe off the gel and asked them to exit through the stairwell. We were looking to see whether or not each participant dropped the paper towel in the stairwell on his or her way towards the exit.

What we found is that when they hadn't viewed an image of themselves before they had the opportunity to litter, about 46 per cent of the participants dropped their towel. But when they had, only about 24 per cent did so. If there's one thing this study does, it helps answer the question, 'How can people who litter look at themselves in the mirror every day?' The answer appears to be that they don't.

In everyday life, we can use mirrors to persuade others with the utmost subtlety to behave in more socially desirable ways. Besides telling us how to arrange our Halloween treats, this research indicates that carefully placed mirrors can encourage kids to act more kindly towards one another. Also, a manager who has experienced employee theft – in the organisation's stockroom, for example – might find that mirrors do wonders in reducing stealing. In this case, mirrors act as a good alternative to video surveillance, which is not only costly but sends a signal to employees that they're not trusted – a prospect that can actually lead to greater employee theft down the line, not less.

If adding mirrors to a specific location isn't practical, there are two other possibilities that produce mirror-like effects. First, social psychologist Ed Diener and his colleagues have found that asking people their names can have a similar effect. This means that asking kids and employees alike to wear name tags should lay the groundwork for more desirable behaviour. Second, recent research by scientist Melissa Bateson and colleagues suggests that placing a simple picture of eyes on the wall also has the effect of getting others to act in more socially conscious ways. For instance, in one study, the researchers added a picture to a communal area where staff members are supposed to drop a certain amount of money into a jar for their coffee or tea consumption. But the signs changed each week: one week, the picture was flowers, the next week it was eyes, then a different set of flowers, then a new set of eyes, and so on. The results showed that coffee and tea drinkers paid over 2.5 times more for their drink when the sign was accompanied by a picture of a pair of eyes than when they saw a picture of flowers.

In sum, whether they're yours or someone else's, it can't hurt to have another pair of eyes looking over the situation.

47

Does being sad make your negotiations bad?

In one episode of the hugely successful television series *Sex and the City*, the main character, Carrie Bradshaw, is walking down a New York City street with close friend Samantha Jones, who is telling Carrie why she's felt so sad recently. At one point in the conversation, Jones, who has been limping along, exclaims, 'Ow!' In response, an empathetic Carrie enquires, 'Honey, if it hurts so much, why are we going shopping?' Samantha retorts, 'I have a broken toe, not a broken spirit.'

Each year, millions of us who feel down seek to alleviate our sorrow through shopping. A recent study conducted by social scientist Jennifer Lerner and her colleagues investigated how emotions such as sadness can deeply affect people's buying – and selling – behaviours, and provided some interesting insights into this phenomenon.

The researchers hypothesised that the experience of sadness motivates people to alter their circumstances, which might help them change their mood. They also thought that this motivation would affect buyers and sellers in different ways: sad buyers would be willing to pay a higher price for a given item than neutral buyers, whereas sad sellers would part with the same item for a lower price than neutral sellers.

In an experiment designed to test these ideas, the researchers induced either sadness or no emotion in their participants by having them view one of two film clips. Those assigned to the sadness-inducing condition watched a clip from the film *The Champ*, which featured the death of a boy's mentor; following that, they were asked to write a brief paragraph about how they'd feel if they'd been in the situation portrayed. Those assigned to the no-emotion condition watched an emotionally neutral film clip featuring fish and then wrote about their day-to-day activities. Afterwards, all participants were told that they were about to take part in a second, unrelated study. Half of the participants were given a set of highlighters and asked to set a price at which to sell them; the other half were asked to set a price at which they would buy them.

The results supported Lerner's assertions. Sad buyers were willing to purchase the item for around 30 per cent *more* than were emotionally neutral buyers. And sad sellers were willing to part with the item for around 33 per cent *less* than were their emotionally neutral counterparts. What's more, the researchers found that the carry-over of the emotion from the film into their economic decisions occurred completely outside the subjects' awareness – they had no idea they had been so deeply affected by these residual feelings of sadness.

How is this research relevant to you? It's extremely important to recognise what emotional state you are in before you make an important decision, begin a crucial negotiation or even respond to an unfriendly e-mail. For example, suppose you have the task of negotiating the financial terms of your contract with a vendor. If you've just gone through an emotional experience, even though you might think your decision-making ability would be unaffected, you should consider holding off on the negotiation process. A short delay will allow time for those emotions to subside, allowing you to make more rational choices.

Whatever the state of your feelings, it would generally be good practice in any high-value decision-making situation to allow a period of time to pass to compose yourself. Often, people schedule meetings back to back as a matter of convenience. By giving yourself a short break in between meetings, however, you'll reduce the likelihood that the feelings generated by an emotionally charged meeting will spill over into the next – especially if the second meeting involves making important decisions.

The same is true of decisions that you might make at home. You might be considering buying some new furniture, a new appliance, some form of home improvement, or even a new home. Or you might be setting prices of items you're planning to sell online. In those situations, it's always wise to take a step back, examine how you feel and put off that activity until you're feeling emotionally neutral.

Finally, those of us looking to influence others' decisions should also be aware of the role that mood plays. Of course, it would be both unwise and wrong to attempt to persuade someone who has just been saddened by a piece of information – or even worse, to bring up some topic that will put the other person in a gloomy mood (e.g. 'Hey, I heard the bad news about your dog. By the way, here's the price I can offer for our deal'). Such decisions will often lead to regret and do little to build long-term relationships. In fact, by offering to postpone nego-tiations with someone who has just had a negative emotional experience, you'll strengthen your relationship by making your-self seem noble, caring and wise, which are priceless character-istics of anyone who wishes to be more persuasive.

48

How can emotion put persuasion in motion?

In 2002, the outbreak of Severe Acute Respiratory Syndrome (better known as SARS) in Asia caused widespread panic and led to plummeting travel to that region. This was the case even though the likelihood of catching SARS, let alone dying from the virus, was extremely small. But what can people's reactions to this event teach us about how emotionally charged issues change people's decision-making and affect the ways they're influenced by others?

Research scientists Christopher Hsee and Yuval Rottenstreich have asserted that people's judgement and decision-making abilities can be impaired by an event such as the SARS outbreak, not because it induces negative feelings, but rather because it is an emotionally charged issue, regardless of the nature of the feelings it produces. Specifically, they argue that emotions lead people to become less sensitive to differences in the *magnitude of numbers*; they're more likely to pay attention to the simple *presence or absence* of an event. In business terms, what this means is that people are more likely to pay attention to the simple presence or absence of an emotion-laden offer than to the specific numbers involved.

To test this idea, the researchers asked participants to spend a brief period of time thinking about some issues either emotionally or non-emotionally. Shortly afterwards, these research subjects were told to imagine that someone they knew was selling a set of Madonna CDs. Half of them were told that there were five CDs in the bundle, whereas the other half were told that there were ten. Participants were then asked to report the maximum amount they'd be willing to pay for the bundle.

The researchers found that those who had earlier practised thinking in an unemotional manner were willing to pay more for the set of ten CDs than for the set of five, which is quite rational. More interestingly, however, those who had earlier practised thinking in an emotional manner were less sensitive to the difference in the number of CDs, reporting that they would pay roughly the same for each set.

The results of this research suggest that emotional experience can have a detrimental impact on decision-making, perhaps allowing you to be persuaded by an offer when you shouldn't be. Suppose that you are negotiating with a supplier for raw materials, and there is a £10,000 gap between the amount of money you are offering and the quantity of the goods the supplier is willing to provide to you for that amount. Recognising this disparity, but not willing to provide any more of those raw materials for the amount you're offering, the supplier might offer to throw in 50 units of a brand-new product that you might be excited about. Whereas it may be the case that 100 units, not 50, are roughly valued at £10,000, this research teaches us that offers laden with emotion such as this one could potentially lead the buyer to overrate the worth of the 50 units, and thus make a poor and unprofitable decision.

How can we prevent these factors from influencing us? The findings from these experiments indicate that doing something as simple as focusing on numbers before the negotiation should help restore your ability to differentiate between the numbers.

Remove the emotions that can cloud your attention, and you will be able to negotiate a deal based on factual, pertinent information and be able to make the best decision possible.

49
What can make people believe everything they read?

A former Chinese political prisoner once described his experiences as a target of brainwashing: 'You are annihilated, exhausted, you can't control yourself, or remember what you said two minutes before. You feel that all is lost. From that moment the judge is the real master of you. You accept *anything* he says' (emphasis added).

To what technique was he referring, and what can this tell us about the factors that allow others to persuade us?

Although the former prisoner was probably the victim of varied thought-reform tactics, the strategy he was referring to was sleep deprivation. Of course, it should come as no surprise that we tend to function better when we have had a good night's sleep. We all know from experience that when we're well rested, we are more focused, we feel more alert and we communicate more eloquently. But work done by social psychologist Daniel Gilbert offers an insight that's less obvious but is completely consistent with the experiences of the political prisoner: we may be more susceptible to others' deceptive influence tactics when we are tired. In a series of studies, Gilbert has found evidence supporting the hypothesis that upon hearing someone else make a statement, the recipient of the message immediately accepts it as true, regardless of whether it is really. It is only with mental effort that, a fraction of a second later, the listener recognises a statement to be false and then rejects it.

When the stakes are high, people usually have enough cognitive resources and motivation to reject statements that sound false. But when people are tired, they're likely to be in a heightened state of gullibility because of the diminished cognitive energy and motivation that exhaustion produces. According to Gilbert's findings, the consequence is that the message comprehension process gets cut off before the rejection stage ever has a chance to take place, making people in this situation more likely to believe others' weak arguments or downright falsehoods. For example, a manager soliciting bids for a big distribution contract would be less likely to question an unlikely statement made by a potential distributor such as 'Our distribution systems are top-rated globally' when operating on little sleep. Instead, he or she is more likely to take this statement at face value.

It's not only sleep deprivation or fatigue which can make us more easily persuaded. Studies also demonstrate that distraction has a similar effect on people's susceptibility to influence, even if that distraction is only momentary. For example, research conducted by Barbara Davis and Eric Knowles found that homeowners were twice as likely to purchase Christmas cards from a door-to-door salesperson when the salesperson distracted them by unexpectedly announcing the price in pennies – rather than the usual dollars – before stating, 'It's a bargain!' Their studies also show that it wasn't simply stating the price in pennies which increased the sales rate: the rate of compliance with the sales pitch was higher than for a standard appeal only when the price was followed by the persuasive statement 'It's a bargain!' The findings reveal that it's during this instant of momentary distraction that the salesperson can slip a persuasive assertion under the radar.

In another study conducted by the same research team, people walking around an outdoor baking sale were more likely to purchase a cupcake when the vendors referred to them as 'half-cakes' rather than 'cupcakes', but only when this was followed by, 'They're delicious!'

What do these studies say about not succumbing to the factors that make us more easily persuaded? The obvious advice is to get more sleep. Of course, we'd all like to get more shut-eye, and we agree that it's easier said than done. If you do happen to find yourself particularly distracted or sleep-deprived, however, try to stay away from programmes such as infomercials, which often make dubious claims. If you don't, you may end up convinced that you really do need an exercise bike that also pops popcorn while you pedal. Instead, try to make important decisions that rely on judgements of the truthfulness of others' claims when you feel most awake.

Next, if you're charged with a task – let's say, for instance, that it's choosing a new supplier – it's good to be aware that you're more likely to believe what you read on a website or formal bid if you're also being distracted, for example by talking on the phone. You're likely to make more accurate evaluations of others' statements and will be generally more resistant to deceptive persuasion tactics if you minimise your distractions. You might, for instance, have a personal 'decision space' at work or home that's free of distractions and background noise so that you can focus on the task at hand. To prevent being first duped (by a double-dealing persuader) and then dumped (by your dissatisfied organisation), it's a good idea to reduce multitasking when the stakes are high.

50

Are tri-meth labs boosting your influence?

Bedwetting, dry mouth and even restless legs. These days, there's seemingly a drug for everything under the sun. You might be surprised to learn, however, that there's a drug called 1,3,7-trimethylxanthin that could make you more persuadable if you take it and more persuasive if you give it to others. Perhaps even more shocking is the fact that this drug is now widely available through 'tri-meth labs' that are popping up in neighbourhoods everywhere.

The drug is more commonly known as caffeine, and these 'tri-meth labs' are more commonly known as coffee shops. Starbucks Corp. alone has over nine thousand locations across 38 countries, although we doubt that chairman Howard Schultz ever dreamt that the beverages he'd make available on every street corner and in every shopping mall could be a potential tool of persuasion. We've all heard – and many of us have experienced – how caffeine can make us feel more alert, but how can it make us more persuasive?

To investigate the question, scientist Pearl Martin and her colleagues first asked all their participants to drink a product resembling orange juice. Like a mischievous teen adding the contents of his flask to the punch bowl at the school disco, the researchers spiked the orange drink before serving it to half of their research subjects. Rather than turning the orange drink into a tequila sunrise, however, the researchers spiked the drink with caffeine – approximately the amount you might find in two cups of espresso.

Shortly after drinking the juice, all the participants read a series of messages containing very good arguments for a certain position on a controversial issue. Those who had consumed the caffeinated beverages prior to reading these arguments were 35 per cent more favourably disposed towards that position than were those who drank the unadulterated drink.

Does this mean that you could walk down to the nearest coffee shop on your lunch break and sell the Brooklyn Bridge to any one of the patrons there? Hardly. In a second study, the researchers also tested the effect of caffeine when participants read messages containing weak arguments. The results showed that under these circumstances caffeine has little persuasive power.

These findings have implications for how you go about making presentations to others, including prospective clients or co-workers. For example, consideration should be given to the time of day you choose to present your information. Let's say that you have a sales presentation to make to a new client. Making your pitch immediately after lunch or later in the day would not be advised. A good time to make your presentation would be earlier in the day, as that's when the clients may have just had their morning coffee fix. Even if you can't choose the time of day, having coffee or caffeinated drinks on hand should make your audience more receptive to your message – provided, as the research suggests, that you make sure your arguments are well reasoned. And, of course, they will be!

Yes!

Influence in the 21st century

As we've moved into the 21st century, our dealings with others within and outside our organisations have changed in two fundamental ways that affect how we persuade others. First, the widespread use of the Internet in home life and in almost every domain of business has caused a massive shift in how we communicate with others on a daily basis. Second, we're more likely than ever now to encounter people in our work environments and our business interactions who are from cultures different from our own. The latest research relating to these rapid transformations will provide you with further invaluable insights into the science of persuasion.

E-influence

Just like any other communications company, US Cellular, a large wireless carrier based in the Midwestern United States, relies almost entirely on technology as the backbone of its business. That's why a policy that the company enacted several years ago seems so ironic, if not completely bonkers: over five thousand employees were told that they were no longer allowed to communicate with one another via e-mail on Fridays.

How could that be possible? In an age in which we're all so

dependent on electronic transmissions to communicate quickly, effectively and accurately with our co-workers, banning e-mail is almost like prohibiting the use of calculators in favour of fingers and toes. Why would US Cellular executive vice-president Jay Ellison issue such a decree? Was it perhaps a nefarious plan concocted by upper management to force employees to run up personal mobile phone bills, thereby increasing short-term profits for the company?

It turns out that after getting bombarded with more e-mails every day than he could open, Ellison started to feel that the endless stream of impersonal, electronic communications might be hurting teamwork and overall productivity, rather than improving it. According to an ABCNews.com report, his memo told employees to 'Get out to meet your teams face-to-face. Pick up the phone and give someone a call ... I look forward to not hearing from any of you, but stop by as often as you like'.

The news report went on to describe some of the dramatic consequences that resulted from the new policy. For example, two co-workers who previously had an e-mail-only relationship were forced to talk to one another by phone. In the course of doing so, they were surprised to learn that they were not in fact across the country from one another, but rather across the hall! This discovery led to face-to-face meetings, which further strengthened their relationship.

Although it no doubt took some time to get accustomed to, the consensus at US Cellular today is that the No E-mail Fridays policy has been a resounding success, and serves as an important reminder about the role that personal interactions with others plays in strengthening our relationships with them. But the case primarily illustrates the impact of electronic interactions on workplace relationships. How do electronic interactions affect our power to persuade?

For example, how might a process like negotiation be affected by whether it takes place online or face to face? Gone are the days when negotiations were conducted exclusively in person or over the phone. Today, more and more negotiations are being conducted online, with the stakes ranging from important terms in a multibillion-dollar contract to the pizza toppings for the office party.

Although the Internet has often been referred to as the information superhighway, might the lack of personal contact between negotiating parties be more like a roadblock than a route to successful outcomes? To test this hypothesis, social scientist Michael Morris and colleagues conducted an experiment in which MBA students engaged in a negotiation task either face to face or via e-mail. The researchers found that negotiating through e-mail made it less likely that the negotiators exchanged the kind of personal information that typically helps establish better rapport, which could ultimately lead to poorer negotiation outcomes.

Behavioural researcher Don Moore and his colleagues thought they might have a pretty simple fix for this potentially not-so-simple problem: what if, prior to the negotiation, the negotiators engaged in some form of mutual self-disclosure? In other words, they could get to know a little bit about one another's background in addition to e-schmoozing for a few minutes on topics unrelated to the negotiation. To test this idea, the researchers paired up students enrolled at two elite US business schools and had them negotiate a deal via e-mail. Whereas half were simply given the instruction to negotiate, the other half were provided with a photograph of the negotiating partner, some brief biographical information about him or her (e.g. undergraduate alma mater, interests) and instructions to spend some time prior to the negotiation getting to know one another through e-mail.

The results of the experiment revealed that when the participants were given no additional information, 29 per cent of the pairs failed to agree on a deal. Only 6 per cent of the more 'personalised' pairs, however, came to an impasse. Using another measure of success, the researchers also found that when the pairs involved in the experiment were able to come to a mutually agreeable negotiated solution, the joint outcome of the settlement – meaning the sum of what each participant walked away with – was 18 per cent higher in the personalised groups as compared with the depersonalised groups. So, by taking the time to learn something personal about your negotiating partner and disclosing something personal about yourself, you'll likely be able to increase the size of the pie for you both to share.

These experiments tell us something about the role of e-communications in negotiations, but what about direct persuasion, where a communicator attempts to shift another person's opinions about a particular idea or issue? In an experiment one of us conducted with lead researcher Rosanna Guadagno, we attempted to address this question. Participants were told that they'd be discussing campus issues in a one-on-one interview with another person, and that they would be doing so either face to face or via e-mail. Unbeknownst to them, the other person was really an undercover research assistant. Using a set script with predetermined arguments, the research assistant tried to persuade the real participant that the university should institute a comprehensive exam policy, meaning that undergraduates would not be able to receive their degree unless they passed a long and difficult exam assessing their knowledge of a broad array of topics. We should note that it's tough to find an issue on which more university students agree. Asking students, with the exception of the occasional egghead, whether they're in favour of requiring comprehensive exams to graduate is like asking them whether they're in favour of a minimum drinking age of 25. Although students initially tend to be almost universally opposed to comprehensive exams, however, it turns out that they can be won round. But does it make a difference whether these persuasive messages are delivered face to face or by e-mail?

The answer depends on the gender of the people involved. Because women are generally more oriented towards building close relationships with their same-sex peers than men, and face-to-face encounters facilitate this process, we predicted that when interacting with a same-sex peer, women would be more persuaded in face-to-face interactions than via e-mail, whereas the form of communication would make less of a difference for men. And that's pretty much what we found: women were more persuaded in person, but men were equally persuaded regardless of the communication medium. Unfortunately, we didn't examine these persuasion differences in opposite-sex pairs, but that may be just as well, as cross-sex persuasion is a topic for a wholly different kind of book!

So far, we've discussed how certain aspects of online communication can act as a roadblock in the building and maintenance of personal relationships. But e-communications can be detrimental to persuasion for a different reason: miscommunications are more likely to occur. And, regrettably, all the strong arguments and effective persuasion strategies in the world aren't going to do you much good if the recipient misunderstands your message, the intentions behind your message or, worse yet, both.

Research conducted by behavioural scientist Justin Kruger and colleagues helps explain why e-mail miscommunications are so commonplace. They suggested that voice inflection and physical gestures – non-verbal cues that are absent in e-mail

– typically act as important indicators of the true meaning of the communication when the content of the message is in any way ambiguous. For example, in response to a message from your colleague concerning vendor contracts, you might write back, 'That's a real priority.' Although you might be completely serious, it's possible that your colleague will interpret this as sarcasm, as you may have objected to the focus on vendor contracts in the past. Had you said it in person, of course, the inflection in your voice, your facial expression and your body language would have made it clear that you were serious. This fact alone is enough to make e-mail communications problematic. But what Kruger and his colleagues argue makes it even more dangerous is that the senders of these messages are almost completely unaware that their messages may be misunderstood. Because the senders have full access to their own intentions when they create their messages, they often assume that the recipient does as well.

The researchers ran a number of experiments to test these hypotheses. In one, participants were grouped into pairs, and each was assigned to be either the conveyer or the recipient of several messages. The communicator's job was to generate several statements that would clearly convey to the recipient one of the following emotions: sarcasm, seriousness, anger or sadness. The participants were also randomly assigned to one of three communication media: e-mail, voice or face-to-face. After each statement was made, the recipient attempted to guess the intended tone of the statement. Also, prior to the task, communicators reported whether or not they thought the recipient would guess correctly.

The results of the study clearly demonstrated that, although communicators in all experimental groups overestimated the extent to which message recipients would correctly interpret their tone, the gap was greatest in the e-mail group. Regardless of experimental group, the communicators anticipated that the recipient would correctly guess the tone about 89 per cent of the time. Whereas those in the voice-only and face-to-face groups were accurate about 74 per cent of the time, however, those in the e-mail group were accurate only about 63 per cent of the time. These results seem to indicate that with written communications in general, because the message recipient can't hear the inflection of the sender's voice, it's harder to interpret his or her message.

You might be thinking to yourself that these findings aren't surprising, considering that these types of experiments almost always involve strangers who have no experience of one another. Surely close friends would be more accurate at interpreting the tone of an e-mail between them? The researchers thought of that, too. Remarkably, the pattern of data looks exactly the same. The fact that written communication can't be fully deciphered even by those close to us suggests that your good friends are wrong when they say they can read you like a book – unless, of course, they're getting you in audiobook format or the made-for-TV-version.

So what's a communicator to do about this hazard? Perhaps you could use 'emoticons', those funny little faces that are intended to convey emotion pictorially (e.g. ':-()'). As seen in this example, however, emoticons can also blend into the rest of the message or be unclear in other ways, resulting in additional confusion. How about eliminating e-mails entirely, choosing to communicate only through phone or face-to-face interactions? That might work once a week, as at US Cellular, but we don't always have the time or ability to engage in those kinds of interactions.

For a potential solution, let's return to one of the central psychological explanations behind these miscommunications. As we alluded to earlier, senders are in a position to know precisely what message they wish to communicate, but they're not naturally inclined to adopt the recipient's perspective. Based on this reasoning, the researchers conducted another experiment to see whether they could eliminate the senders' overconfidence that their messages would be understood as intended. This experiment was similar in design to the guess-the-tone one we described a moment ago, with a few variations. First, all participants communicated with one another solely via e-mail. Second, some participants were given instructions designed to make them consider how their statements could be misinterpreted. The researchers found that this group of participants increased their accuracy in predicting whether their messages would be understood as intended.

So, based on the findings of this experiment, how can we become more effective e-communicators and therefore increase our online persuasion skills? Before sending e-mails to others on any topic of importance, it would be wise to take a moment to read through the message with an eye to how certain aspects of the message could potentially be interpreted differently by the recipient, so that you can change the message to clarify what you mean. In other words, just as you might use spell-checking or grammar-checking to improve the clarity of your message before irrevocably hitting that 'Send' button, perspective-taking can make your message better understood. If you're reading this, Bill Gates, it's too late – we're already working on the patents.

Finally, we should note that even if the recipients of your messages fully understand your intentions, that certainly doesn't guarantee that they'll comply with your requests or come to your aid if you ask them to. To give just one example, a medical doctor we know had great difficulty trying to get someone to cover his shift so that he could attend a wedding. It was perplexing to us because he is such a likeable and well-respected person, and we know he had covered for several of his colleagues in the past. But when we enquired how exactly he went about asking for his colleagues' help, we knew instantly what the problem was: he told us he had sent out a mass e-mail with the request, in which everyone could see the names of all the other recipients.

The problem with this strategy is that it produces what's called *diffusion of responsibility*. By sending out the mass e-mail in a way that made visible the large number of colleagues being asked, no one felt personally responsible for helping – instead, they all probably assumed that *someone else* on the list would agree to help. In a classic demonstration of diffusion of responsibility, social psychologists John Darley and Bibb Latané staged a situation in which a student appeared to be having an epileptic seizure. When a lone bystander was present, that person helped roughly 85 per cent of the time. But when there were five bystanders – all of whom were located in separate rooms, so no one could be sure whether the victim was receiving help – only 31 per cent of the bystanders provided assistance.

So, what could our friend have done to increase the odds that someone would volunteer to cover his shift? If he had the time, he could have picked out the people who he felt would be most likely to say yes – perhaps those he had covered for in the past – and either asked them in person or sent them personalised e-mails requesting their help. Or, if those weren't viable options for some reason, he could have at least sent some people a blind carbon copy so that others weren't fully aware of how many people had been asked.

So far we've discussed how the process of communicating with and influencing others is affected by using e-mail as opposed to more traditional forms of communication. But what about other aspects of e-persuasion? For example, how might psychological research bear on how to design your business's website? Let's start with an illustration.

Suppose that one day, after reading this book, you decide that you want to own two more copies of it – so you have one for your home, one for the office and one for the glove compartment in case of emergencies.

After you have grabbed the last two copies of *Yes!* from the shelf at a local bookshop and brought them to the till, you are taken aback by something the shop's employee says. 'Are you sure you want to buy those books here?' he asks. 'I know we have one of the more competitive prices on that book, but the bookshop just down the street is selling it for about fifteen per cent less. If you'd like, I can draw you a map of how to get there.' With customer service like that – or, more accurately, with *non*-customer service like that – you wonder how this place is still standing.

Although this example may sound somewhat absurd, some businesses have adopted this seemingly self-exterminating practice. For instance, take Progressive Auto Insurance, the third-largest motor insurance company in the United States. The company has always prided itself on innovations that distinguish it from its competitors, including being the first major insurance company in the world to launch a website, in 1995. One year later, car owners searching for insurance rates could use the website not only to learn about Progressive's rates, but also to learn about the rates offered by the company's major competitors. Today, the home page even features a 'rate ticker', a scrolling information bar listing the comparisons that recent visitors learned about. Although Progressive clearly has the better rates in many of these instances, this is not always the case. For example, when we checked the site one minute before writing this, the rate ticker revealed that someone with the initials C.M. in the US state of Wisconsin would save almost $942 per year by insuring his or her Toyota with one of Progressive's competitors.

So, is Progressive insuring more customers with this strategy, or is it ensuring its own extinction? The company's enormous growth since it implemented this innovation – an average of 17 per cent a year, with annual premiums growing from $3.4 billion to $14 billion – suggests it's working. Research by Valerie Trifts and Gerald Häubl may explain why.

In their experiment, Trifts and Häubl told research participants that their university was considering a joint venture with one of several online book retailers. The participants' job was to do an online search for a set list of books, compare the books' prices among the different retailers and decide which retailer to buy from. Importantly, for half of the participants a certain retailer listed not only its own price for a given book but also the prices of a number of other booksellers, whereas it didn't provide this comparison for the other half of the participants. The researchers also varied that retailer's market position, meaning that some participants saw that the retailer's prices, on average, were relatively low, others saw that they were relatively high, and yet others saw that they were about even with the other retailers.

Did the results support Progressive's practices? To a large extent, they did, but it's important to note that the results depended on the critical factor of market position. When the prices of the Progressive-like retailer in question were clearly and consistently below or above those of the others, it didn't really matter whether or not the price comparison was provided. When, however, the Progressive-like retailer's prices were higher for some of the books and lower for others – which is closer to how most businesses operate in the real world – providing the comparison made the difference: participants in this situation reported being more likely to shop with the Progressive-like retailer. Besides appearing more trustworthy – after all, as we discussed earlier in the book, dishonest people and organisations rarely argue against their self-interest – consumers probably appreciate having the price comparisons in one place, as it saves them both time and effort.

In sum, to return to the original bookshop scenario, the results of this study – and of Progressive's success to date with this practice – suggest that companies that provide potential customers with their competitors' prices may occasionally lose the battle but are definitely poised to win the pricing war.

The research on online comparisons showed how certain features of a business's website can be crafted to persuade potential customers to use its services. But are there less obvious aspects of web pages that can influence consumer behaviour? For example, could something as subtle as your web page's background turn your potential customers from browsers into buyers?

Several experiments conducted by consumer researchers Naomi Mandel and Eric Johnson suggest the answer is yes. In one of those experiments, participants visited a web page that housed a hypothetical shopping site on which they had to choose between two sofas. One sofa was described as very comfortable but also very expensive, whereas the other was described as only somewhat comfortable but inexpensive. The researchers also varied the web page's background to try to shift the participants' decision-making towards saving money or towards comfort. In choosing the backgrounds, they relied on some data from a previous study, in which participants were shown an ad for a sofa that had one of two possible backgrounds: either pictures of pennies against a green backdrop or pictures of fluffy clouds against a blue backdrop. After asking the participants to generate a list of the most important aspects to consider when buying a sofa, participants who viewed the penny background were more likely to cite the importance of cost than those who viewed the clouds background. In a similar vein, those who viewed the clouds background were more likely to highlight comfort than those who viewed the penny background.

In view of these preliminary findings, Mandel and Johnson suspected that when participants shopped for a sofa at an online store featuring the cloud-filled background, they would be more likely to buy the more comfortable (but more expensive) sofa, whereas the reverse would be true for the penny-filled background – and that's exactly what they found. These results weren't limited to a single type of product, either. For example, participants were more likely to choose the safer (but more expensive) car over the less safe (but less expensive) car when the background was a red-and-orange image reminiscent of flames that you might see in a car crash.

What's particularly remarkable about these findings is how powerfully but subtly these cues influence people's behaviour. For example, nearly all the participants in these experiments insisted that the backgrounds had no effect whatsoever on their choices. Yet, as we know, these views simply don't reflect reality.

Perhaps the most important implication of these findings is that certain aspects of your company's web page, such as the images presented in the background, have a far greater influence on consumers' behaviour than you might think. They suggest that you can strategically choose the backgrounds and other images on your website based on the strengths of your goods and services. In other words, by carefully selecting your site's background, you can bring your products' strengths – and perhaps also those of your organisation – into the foreground.

Global influence

Hai. Hao. Da. Ja. Sí. Oui. People from around the globe say *yes* in very different ways, but does that mean that the persuasion strategies we use to get them to say it should differ depending on the message recipient's cultural background? Or is a one-size-fits-all approach likely to be equally effective regardless of where a person comes from? Although the fundamental princi-ples of social influence and many of the strategies we discuss throughout this book are powerful persuaders in all cultures, recent research suggests that there are some subtle differences in how you should tailor your tactics and your messages to the cultural background of the person you're trying to persuade. In essence, these differences result from variations in cultural norms and traditions, which lead the people of different socie-ties to place greater weight on some aspects of a persuasive message than on others.

Take, for example, research conducted by Michael Morris and colleagues, who studied the employees of Citibank, one of the world's largest multinational financial corporations. Morris and colleagues surveyed Citibank branches in four different countries – the United States, Germany, Spain and China (Hong Kong) – and measured employees' willingness to comply volun-tarily with a request from a co-worker for help with a task. Although the survey respondents were influenced by many of the same factors, some factors were more influential than others in the different countries.

Employees in the United States, for instance, were most likely to take an approach based on direct reciprocation. They asked the question, 'What has this person done for me?' and felt obligated to volunteer if they owed the requester a favour. German employees, on the other hand, were most likely to be influenced by whether or not the request stayed within the rules of the organisation. They decided whether to comply by asking, 'According to official regulations and categories, am I supposed to assist this requester?' Spanish Citibank personnel based the decision mostly on friendship norms that encourage loyalty to one's friends, regardless of position or status. They asked, 'Is this requester connected to my friends?' And finally, Chinese employees responded primarily to authority in the form of loyalties to those of high status within their small group. They asked, 'Is this requester connected to someone in my unit, especially someone who is high-ranking?'

As Morris and his colleagues point out, there are several important practical implications of this research. For one, businesses looking to transfer practices, policies and organisational structures from one cultural setting to the next need to be sensitive to the obligation norms of the new culture – or risk turning what may be a well-oiled machine in one society into a gunk-filled clunker in the next.

The results also suggest that managers who move from one cultural setting to another may need to adjust the strategies they use to secure compliance from others in their branch. For example, a manager who is transferred from Munich to an office in Madrid may find that developing personal friendships with others becomes an increasingly important aspect of gaining compliance in the new workplace. A manager who makes the reverse shift, however, may find that making requests outside the organisation's formal guidelines – for instance, asking a co-worker to bypass some paperwork, perhaps an accepted practice in her former work environment – isn't considered appropriate in her new location.

Although the four cultures examined in the Citibank research differ on several important psychological dimensions, social influence researchers have focused their attention on how one particular dimension, known as individualism-collectivism, affects the persuasion process. In brief, individualism is an orientation that assigns the highest priority to the preferences and rights of the individual. Collectivism, on the other hand, assigns the highest priority to the preferences and rights of the group. Although it's something of an oversimplification, one might say that in individualistic cultures it's more about *me*, whereas in collectivistic cultures it's more about *we*. People in countries like the United States, the United Kingdom and others in western Europe tend to be more individualistic. In contrast, many other countries around the globe, including those that are now burgeoning areas for international business partnerships – those in Asia, South America, Africa and eastern Europe – are more collectivistic.

Researchers Sang-Pil Han and Sharon Shavitt set out to examine the implications of these different cultural orientations for persuasion in a marketing context. Their prediction was that in collectivistic cultures, advertisements that focus consumers on the product's benefits to one's group members (e.g. friends, family or co-workers) would be more persuasive than advertisements that focus consumers solely on the product's benefits for the consumer him- or herself. They also thought that this would be especially likely for products that are typically shared with others, such as air conditioners or toothpaste.

Han and Shavitt first looked for evidence to support their

ideas. They picked two magazines in the USA and two in South Korea, making sure that they matched the magazines in the two countries on popularity and genre. They then randomly selected advertisements from those magazines and had trained native and bilingual speakers evaluate them for the extent to which they focused readers on the benefit of the product to themselves or on its benefit to their group. The researchers found that the US ads were indeed more likely than South Korean ads to highlight how the products' benefits were conferred on the individual, especially when compared with products that were shared with others. Whereas the US advertisements tended to appeal to the reader's individuality (e.g. 'the art of being unique'), motivation for self-improvement (e.g. 'You, only better') and personal goals (e.g. 'With this new look I'm ready for my new role'), the South Korean ads tended to appeal to the reader's sense of responsibility to the group (e.g. 'A more exhilarating way to provide for your family'), motivation to enhance the group (e.g. 'the dream of prosperity for all of us') and consideration of the group's opinions (e.g. 'Our family agrees with the selection of home furnishings').

After confirming that the persuasive messages embedded in these ads targeted different consumer motivations based on the cultural orientation of the society, the researchers wanted to answer a more psychologically important question: are collectivistic- and individualistic-oriented messages actually more persuasive in their respective cultures? After all, as we discussed in the Introduction, the fact that marketers think certain types of messages will be most effective doesn't simply make them so.

To answer this question, Han and Shavitt created two versions of advertisements for a variety of products – one version more individualistic-oriented, the other more collectivistic-oriented. For example, the individualistic version of an ad for a brand of chewing gum ran, 'Treat yourself to a breath-freshening experience.' Notice that this message is focused on the breath-freshening benefits as they affect solely the consumer. But, as we all know from experience, the state of a person's breath isn't solely a personal issue; it can affect those around that person as well. Understandably, then, the more collectivistic version of this ad stated, 'Share the breath-freshening experience.' (Of course, the ads were written in English for the US participants and in Korean for the South Korean participants.)

The results revealed that South Korean participants were more persuaded by the collectivistic than the individualistic ad, and for US participants the reverse was true. And, consistent with the earlier study, this effect was especially powerful with products that people tend to share with others. This should give pause to any marketer considering blanketing various countries with a one-strategy-fits-all marketing campaign. Instead, such campaigns should be tailored to fit the cultural orientation of the societies in which they take place. The breath of an entire nation may depend on it.

The Han and Shavitt research shows how people from individualistic cultures tend to give greater consideration to their own experiences, whereas people from collectivistic cultures tend to give greater consideration to the experiences of others close to them. How might these cultural differences affect the relative weight that people give to the fundamental principles of social influence?

To open up this question, let's consider an example. And who better to illustrate the tendencies of people in an individualistic-oriented culture than a prominent figure from the most individualistic of countries – the USA – and from the most individualistic of sports – golf. Several years ago, legendary US golfer

Jack Nicklaus witnessed the heartbreaking death of his young grandson. Several days later, Nicklaus made it clear in an interview that his chances of playing in one of golf's most prestigious events, the Masters, were 'between slim and none'. Yet, to the surprise of many, he also announced that he would play in two other golf outings in the near future. What powerful factor could convince a grieving man to participate in these events after being stricken by such tragedy?

It turns out that Nicklaus had promised to play in each event before his grandson passed away. As the golfer put it, 'You make commitments, and you've got to do them.' As we have discussed, the motivation to be consistent with one's commitments can be powerful in influencing a person's actions. But does it motivate with the same force equally across cultures? All else being equal, would a golfer from a different cultural background feel just as bound by his or her previous actions and commitments in the same situation?

To help get a better understanding of the answer to this question, let's consider an experiment that one of us conducted with Stephen Sills and lead researcher Petia Petrova. In this study, students who were native to the United States and Asian international students received an e-mail that asked them to complete an online survey. A month after receiving the first request, each received an e-mail requesting participation in an online survey related to the first project, which they were told would take about twice as long to complete as the original survey.

So what did we find? First off, we found that US students were slightly less likely to comply with the initial request than were their Asian counterparts. Yet, of those who did comply with the initial request, the US participants were more likely to comply with the second request (around 22 per cent) than the

Asian participants (around 10 per cent). Put another way, we found that compliance with the initial request had a far greater influence on subsequent compliance among US participants than among Asian participants.

Why was this the case? Perhaps another study might shed more light on this perplexing question, research that one us of conducted with several colleagues. In this study, we found that when we asked American students to participate without pay in a marketing survey, they were more influenced by their own history of agreement to such requests – in other words, their prior commitments – than by their peers' history of agreement. But in Poland, a more collectivistic-oriented country, precisely the opposite was the case. In Poland what a student's peer group had previously done was a more powerful motivator of current compliance than what the student had done.

These findings are primarily due to cultural differences in individualism and collectivism. Because people from individualistic cultures tend to give greater weight to their personal experiences, consistency with one's previous experiences is often a more potent motivator for them. And because people from collectivistic cultures tend to give greater weight to the experiences of others close to them, the behaviour of those others is often a more powerful motivator for them. What this means is that when asking a Briton, an American or a Canadian for a favour, you will be more successful by pointing out that it fits with what that person has done before. But when asking a favour of people from more collectivistic countries, you will be more successful by pointing out that it fits with what that person's peer group has done before.

To take a specific example, suppose your company has been doing business successfully with a firm in eastern Europe for two years. During that time, you have often had to ask your

European partners for the favour of providing updated marketing information. Your main contact there, Slawek, and his co-workers have usually gone out of their way to help you. Suppose further that you need updated information once more and that in a phone conversation you make your request as follows: 'Slawek, you have been so helpful in the past that I'm hoping you can provide us with updated information again.' In so doing, you will have made a mistake. The results of these studies suggest that you would have had more success if you had said, 'Slawek, you *and your co-workers* have been so helpful in the past that I'm hoping you can provide us with updated information again.' It's an easy mistake for a British, western European or North American person to make because those individuals assume that everyone prefers to operate according to the principle of personal consistency – the tendency to decide what one should do based on what one has previously done. But, as these studies demonstrated, in many collectivistic countries personal consistency with one's prior actions is outweighed by the principle of social proof – the tendency to decide what one should do based on what one's group has previously done.

People from collectivistic and individualistic cultures also tend to differ in the relative weight they give to two central functions of communication. In short, one function of communication is informational: when we communicate, we convey information to others. A second, less obvious function is relational: when we communicate, we help build and maintain relationships with others. Although both functions are clearly important to people in all cultures, researchers Yuri Miyamoto and Norbert Schwarz have suggested that individualistic cultures place a greater emphasis on the informational function of communication, whereas collectivistic cultures place a greater emphasis on the relational function.

Although this cultural difference has implications for a variety of communication-related issues, Miyamoto and Schwarz examined one aspect of communication that permeates our daily lives at home and in the workplace – leaving phone messages for others. The researchers suspected that because people from Japan tend to be collectivistic and therefore more focused on forming and maintaining relationships with others, they would have a harder time making a somewhat complex request on an answering machine. They reasoned that if Japanese people care more about how their communications affect their relationship with message recipients than Americans, conveying a message in which they receive no feedback as to how it is being received should cause them more mental fatigue. To test this, Miyamoto and Schwarz had American and Japanese participants leave a somewhat detailed request for help on an answering machine using their native languages. Whereas the Americans cut right to the heart of the information, their Japanese counterparts took longer to leave their messages, seeming to be more concerned about how their message would affect their relationship with the recipient.

The researchers also surveyed Japanese and American participants about their experiences with answering machines. Whereas Americans reported hanging up when reaching an answering machine about half the time, Japanese people reported hanging up an astounding 85 per cent of the time. And, consistent with the researchers' explanation for the results of the previous study, when asked what they disliked most about answering machines, the Japanese respondents were more likely to cite relational reasons (e.g. 'It is hard to sound personal on the answering machine') than were Americans, whereas the cultural pattern was reversed for informational reasons (e.g. 'People sometimes don't check it').

What do these findings say about influencing others in and out of the workplace? As we discussed earlier in this section, relationships are a key component of the persuasion process – but this is especially true with people from countries with collectivistic orientations. When leaving messages for others, it can be tempting, especially to people from individualistic cultures, to focus entirely on efficiently conveying a piece of information while ignoring one's relationship with the message receiver. These results suggest that, when dealing with people from collectivistic cultures, it is particularly important to attend to your relationship – and in particular to attributes that you genuinely share.

The same should apply to conversations. In fact, based on some research showing how Japanese listeners tend to provide more feedback (e.g. 'I see', 'Yes') than their American counterparts during conversations, Miyamoto and Schwarz suggest that a Japanese person might find talking to an American somewhat akin to talking to an answering machine. This idea fits with an additional survey finding that Japanese participants were more likely to say that they disliked answering machines because 'It is hard to speak because there are no responses'. These findings suggest that we should be sure to provide such feedback with people from collectivistic cultures, letting them know that we're attending to the relationship that we share with them as well as to the information they're trying to convey.

The results also serve as a warning that 'letting the call go to voicemail' can be a treacherous decision, especially when the caller is from a collectivistic culture. If you think that the worst that can happen is that you get yourself into a simple game of 'phone tag', you may find that it soon becomes a single-player game.

Yes!

Ethical influence

Throughout this book, we've described social influence strategies that we've referred to as tools for your persuasion toolbox. And that's exactly how they should be used – as constructive tools that help build authentic relationships with others, highlight the genuine strengths of one's message, initiative or product, and ultimately create outcomes that are in the best interests of all parties. When these tools are instead used unethically as weapons, however – for example, by dishonestly or artificially importing the principles of social influence into situations in which they don't naturally exist – the short-term gains will almost invariably be followed by long-term losses. Although the dishonest use of persuasion strategies may occasionally work in the short run – perhaps someone could be persuaded with a bad set of arguments or could be tricked into buying a defective product – the long-term reputational consequences are dire when such dishonesty is eventually discovered.

It's not simply the dishonest use of persuasion tools which people would be wise to avoid; there are also inherent dangers in trying to exploit the applications of some of the tools that we've described. For example, in the spring of 2000 the UK found itself in the midst of a serious crisis. Businesses up and down the country were crying out in desperation; schools were deserted; shops were struggling to find customers; and public services were at risk of a meltdown. The reason for the crisis? There was no petrol. Actually, that last statement is only partially true. There was plenty of petrol; it was just that stations had no supplies owing to the blockading of a number of oil refineries by protesters who were upset about how much they had to pay at the pump.

The shortage quickly had an impact. Tens of thousands of motorists formed queues outside petrol stations to fill up with much-needed supplies. As the shortage began to take a grip, the behaviour of the motorists changed. Local and national newspapers, radio stations and TV channels ran stories describing how car owners would join one queue to fill their tanks with petrol, only to drive a few miles down the road and join another one to top up their tanks again. Other drivers slept overnight in their cars outside garage forecourts, hoping they might be the lucky recipients of one of the rare shipments of fuel that did get through the blockades. This is the power of scarcity in action.

At the height of the crisis, there was a garage owner who had reportedly received a supply of much-needed fuel. In fact, he was the only garage owner for many miles around with supplies of petrol, and the news quickly spread. Recognising the unique position in which he found himself, seeing the lengthy queue forming outside, this enterprising businessman, perhaps unsurprisingly, took advantage of his situation by adding a premium to the price of his petrol. But instead of adding a small amount, he increased his prices tenfold, to over £6 per litre!

Did the disgruntled but still petrol-hungry motorists refuse en masse to pay such extortionate prices? Hardly. Although they were angry, they still lined up in droves to get whatever petrol they could. In a matter of hours, the last drop of petrol was drained from the station's tank, and the owner made a profit in a single day that would have normally taken him two weeks.

But what happened to his business two weeks later, after the crisis had ended? In a word, the consequences were disastrous. By exploiting the scarcity of petrol and forcing desperate drivers to pay ridiculously inflated prices, he profited in the short term but completely lost out in the long run. People simply boycotted his business. Some went further, making it their goal to inform their friends, neighbours and co-workers about the owner's actions. His business lost nearly every customer it had, and within a very short time his damaged reputation forced him to close. This is completely consistent with an abundance of research showing that those who behave in an untrustworthy matter can do little to regain the public's trust.

If the owner had considered the set of powerful social influence tools available to him in his persuasion toolbox, he would have found that there were certainly better choices available – choices that could have led to far greater profits in the long term. For one thing, he could have ensured that his petrol supplies went primarily to his local or regular customers, making a point of informing them that he did so because he valued their loyalty. Or he could have put up a sign saying that he refused to fleece needy motorists in a time of crisis; acting against his own self-interest (at least his short-term self-interest) in this way certainly would have made him more likeable, generous and trustworthy in the motorists' eyes, a move that surely would have paid big dividends in the future. Even if he had done nothing but keep the prices reasonable, customers would probably have been more than happy to buy some extras from the shop just because they felt grateful that he wasn't taking advantage of them under those trying circumstances.

In a way, though, the garage owner's actions are understandable. In the same way that many of the people we wish to influence are often forced to make decisions quickly by the fast-paced world around them, the same is true for us as persuaders. Often the first influence strategy that comes to mind will not be the most ethical. But by taking the extra effort to consider all the options that are now available to you – using your new toolbox – you can move people towards your perspective, product or initiative in a way that's genuine, honest and long-lasting. And at the same time, as ethical persuaders, we can take comfort in knowing that those who choose to wield social influence as a weapon, rather than a tool, will inevitably end up shooting themselves in the foot.

Yes!

Influence in action

In this book we've attempted to discuss a number of insights into how the influence process works from a scientific perspective. We've been vigilant in providing only the influence strategies that have been shown, through rigorously controlled studies and research, to be effective. We deliberately haven't based our recommendations on our own hunches or anecdotes. Instead, we've relied entirely on the significant body of research from the study of social influence and persuasion. Accordingly, you can be confident that your attempts to influence and persuade others no longer need to be based solely on your intuitions and experiences. You now have science on your side, too.

We're frequently contacted by people who report to us their experiences of using the science of persuasion. These people come from many types of work settings. Some work for multinational corporations, others work in government or education, others are self-employed – and yet others are people who are simply interested in what science tells us about how to be persuasive. Here are just a few examples of how they ethically employed one or more scientific insights in a way that has helped them become more persuasive.

Nick Pope, Director of Salesforce Training (Europe, Middle East, Africa), Bausch and Lomb:

One way we develop relationships with customers is to invite them to educational presentations and meetings. These days, our customers are bombarded with requests to attend meetings and study days that are sponsored by different companies. It's no wonder that sometimes many of those who initially say they will attend an event do not actually turn up. This can have a significant impact on our business.

Using the principle of commitment and consistency, before we invite any customers to an important meeting, we ask them (a) to register their interest on a particular subject and then (b) to create a few questions that they would like answered on the topic.

When they receive their invite we make it clear that some of these questions will be answered by our guest speaker and expert on the topic.

The expectation that their question (which they have already committed to asking) could be asked in an open forum has seen participant levels dramatically increase since using this principle.

Dan Norris, Director of Training, Holt Development Services, San Antonio, Texas:

Giveaways are a hallmark of the sports franchise world. Be it bobble hats, T-shirts or free seats, many teams like ours use them to lure fans to games. The owner of our company owns several sports teams, including a minor league hockey club.

After a period of low ticket sales, we had to report to our season ticket holders that we had to cut back our promotional giveaways. We scheduled several focus groups, and the first group reacted very negatively to the news. They almost viewed the giveaways as an expectation rather than as a gift. We inadvertently had them focus on the possibility of losing the very things they had come to expect. The meeting quickly spiralled downward, and many fans went home angry.

Afterwards, we met to discuss a different strategy, and thought about how we could be more effective by applying the principle of reciprocity. At our next focus group meeting, we started off by asking the fans to name the different giveaways we'd offered over the years. They began to call out answers like jerseys, extra tickets, autographed hockey sticks, etc. We followed up their answers by saying, 'We are happy we have been able to provide those gifts to you in the past, and would like to continue to do so in the future. However, our ticket sales are falling and that will make that difficult. What can we do together to help bring in more fans to the games?' The reaction couldn't have been more different from the first group. The fans began collaborating on how they could get more of their friends and family members to attend the games, and some even remarked, 'It's the least we can do after all of the great things you've done for us.'

John Fisher, Preston, UK:

My wife had her own business making and selling children's clothes. When she first started up she only had a few styles and fabric patterns to offer to her customers. As her business started to grow and she attracted new customers she decided to expand the range she offered both in terms of the style of the children's clothes and also the fabrics and patterns she offered. We consistently found that the more choice people had the less they bought. Whilst, like most people, we would consider more choice to be a good thing, my wife found that having lots of options for her customers often meant they did less business with her.

Brian F. Ahearn, State Auto Insurance Companies,
Columbus, Ohio:

One of my responsibilities is to help recruit new independent agencies to represent our company. In our effort to do this we sent marketing materials to prospective agencies so they could learn more about us. While we hope most agents read our communications, seldom did we receive any direct replies. After learning about the principle of scarcity we realised we were missing out on an opportunity that had been right in front of us all along!

We don't do business in every state and each year we set a modest goal for appointing new agents in our operating areas. We never thought to incorporate those facts, or our current progress, into the communications we were sending. Understanding how scarcity can move people to action we began to include something like this near the end of our communications: 'Each year we have a goal of selecting just a few new agencies to partner with us. For 2006 that number has been set at only 42 agencies across our 28 operating states and so far we've appointed more than 35. It's our sincere hope that your agency will be one of those remaining agencies we appoint before year-end.'

The difference was noticeable immediately! Within days we began to receive enquiries. No extra cost, no new marketing campaigns, no product or system changes needed. The only change was adding three more sentences that contain true statements.

Kathy Fragnoli, Resolutions Group, Dallas and San Diego:

I am an attorney who left the practice of law thirteen years ago to become a full-time mediator. My job is to meet with parties who are involved in litigation and help them settle their disputes. Most are represented by lawyers. A typical mediation starts with all of the parties in one room. Each is asked to provide a statement of their case. After opening statements, I escort each side to their respective rooms and I go back and forth between them in an effort to persuade each litigant that the position they took early in the morning needs to shift for the case to settle. I often provide private input on the strengths and weaknesses of each case to facilitate movement.

Before reading about the psychology of persuasion I would allow the parties to state their monetary demands in the opening session for the other party to hear. Once I understood the principle of consistency, however, I began requesting that each side hold off on their monetary demands or offers until I met with them privately. My settlement rate increased dramatically when I realised that the public commitment to a number was hindering the effort to compromise. I quickly realised that the more people in the room heard the opening demands, the harder it was to move them away from their positions!

Dil Sidhu, *Acting Assistant Chief Executive, London Borough of Lambeth:*

When I moved to this office, the borough had major problems with operations, leadership and managing change and was undergoing a major recovery programme. By using the principle of authority (which maintains that people rely on those with superior knowledge or wisdom for guidance on how to respond) I found useful ways of ensuring that the government monitoring and advisory panel were accepting of the type and speed of change being achieved. I ensured that the credentials of the people brought in to work on the turnaround were well publicised along with the names of other organisations where they were instrumental in improving performance. A small thing, but it elicited a huge attitude change from the advisory panel and allowed us the freedom to get on with the job of recovery.

Christy Farnbauch, Hilliard City Schools, Hilliard, Ohio:

I had the opportunity to put some of the principles to the test during a school bond campaign. I work for the ninth-largest school district in Ohio and we tried, unsuccessfully, three times to pass a bond levy that would provide funding for a third high school and fourteenth elementary school. During the last campaign (Feb–May 2006), I suggested that we try some new tactics based on the science of persuasion.

We chose a campaign theme worded in the negative: 'Our Kids Can't Wait'. In the past, campaign themes had always been positive (i.e. Unite for Kids, Building Tomorrow Today, etc.). We were trying to communicate a sense of limited time to do the right thing and touch on loss aversion. The implication was – our kids (and the community) will lose if we don't act now. We developed three clear messages, based on community research, and clearly articulated those messages over and over (a proven political strategy). We also built a social network of over 10,000 voters by using a Get Out the Vote strategy called 'Mine +9'. Through a phone survey, the most likely supportive voters were identified and 1,000 volunteers were asked to choose nine names of people who were their friends and/or colleagues to call and follow up with over a three-week period prior to the election. The volunteers were well informed. Many volunteers were 'convert communicators' who had voted against previous levies. The potential voters were asked to make a commitment to voting on the school issue and were simultaneously held accountable by a friend or colleague. They received reminders about the election right up until the polls closed on election day. We also created campaign postcards and other communications that were tailored to specific areas throughout the district. Again, a first.

While I can't scientifically prove that any of these strategies helped us win the election, we did pass the issue with a wide margin. I believe that these tactics were invaluable to our success and we will use them again for future campaigns.

Tim Batchelor, training manager, Surrey:

Whilst in the role of Head of Training at a major pharmaceutical company I had the responsibility of launching a new Presentation Skills Programme to our 400 UK sales staff. Whilst we knew that the programme was very innovative we also knew that not everyone would think the same as us about the initiative. A lot of the staff had been in the organisation for some years and probably thought they had seen it all before. Based on the idea that people follow the lead of lots of others like them, in the first couple of workshops we asked people to write down one thing they genuinely liked about the workshop. We took that good feedback and printed it on large posters which we displayed on the walls at future events. In fact before we started any training we asked delegates to review the posters and see what their colleagues were saying about the programme. I was a little sceptical at first about whether such a simple thing would work but the impact was incredible. By the end of the programme we had collected over 200 e-mails from people who had attended (an unprecedented number). What was interesting was that this catalogue of testimonials also helped me to influence senior managers to support future projects I was leading. After all, it wasn't just me telling them how great the Training Department was. I now had the written testimonials of 200 staff saying so as well.

Influence At Work

We would be delighted to hear from readers of this book who submit an example of their own use of ethical influence for possible inclusion in future editions. Please send them to the relevant contact below or submit them via our websites. And for more information about Influence At Work, who provide training and consultancy services based on the strategies in this book, please contact:

In the United States, Canada and the rest of the world	In the UK and Europe
Influence At Work	Influence At Work (UK)
The Broadmor Place	Dixies Barn D, High Street
2248 South Forest Avenue	Ashwell
Tempe, AZ 85252	Hertfordshire SG7 5NT
United States of America	United Kingdom
+1 (0) 480 967 6070	+44 (0) 870 787 4747
info@influenceatwork.com	info@influenceatwork.co.uk
www.influenceatwork.com	www.influenceatwork.co.uk

You can receive our free monthly *Inside Influence Report Newsletter* by visiting www.influenceatwork.com or www.influenceatwork.co.uk.

Research notes

Introduction

The full reference for Robert Cialdini's book is: Cialdini, R. B. (2001), *Influence: Science and Practice* (4th edn), Boston, MA: Allyn & Bacon.

1 How can you increase your persuasiveness by inconveniencing your audience?

The staring-upwards study can be found in: Milgram, S., L. Bickman and L. Berkowitz (1969), 'Note on the drawing power of crowds of different size', *Journal of Personality and Social Psychology*, 13: 79–82.

The hotel study data are from a manuscript currently undergoing the peer review process: Goldstein, N. J., R. B. Cialdini and V. Griskevicius (2007), 'A room with a viewpoint: the role of situational similarity in motivating conservation behaviours', Manuscript submitted for publication.

For those interested in learning more about why there's good reason to follow crowds, see: Surowiecki, J. (2005), *The Wisdom of Crowds*, New York: Doubleday.

2 What shifts the bandwagon effect into another gear?

For an interesting set of experiments examining how we automatically associate certain behaviours with specific environments and situations, see: Aarts, H. and A. Dijksterhuis (2003), 'The silence of the library: environment, situational norm, and social behaviour', *Journal of Personality and Social Psychology*, 84: 18–28.

The hotel study data reported in this chapter are from the same hotel study manuscript described in the previous chapter.

3 What common mistake causes messages to self-destruct?

You can view these two public service announcements on the Keep America Beautiful Organisation's website at the following address: www.kab.org/media.asp?id=246&rid=250.

The national park data were published in: Cialdini, R. B. (2003), 'Crafting normative messages to protect the environment', *Current Directions in Psychological Science*, 12: 105–109.

For more on the Petrified Forest studies, see: Cialdini, R. B., L. J. Demaine, B. J. Sagarin, D. W. Barrett, K. Rhoads and P. L. Winter (2006), 'Managing social norms for persuasive impact', *Social Influence*, 1: 3–15.

4 When persuasion might backfire, how do you avoid the 'magnetic middle'?

The household energy conservation study can be found in: Schultz, P. W., J. M. Nolan, R. B. Cialdini, N. J. Goldstein and V. Griskevicius (2007), 'The constructive, destructive, and reconstructive power of social norms', *Psychological Science*, 18: 429–34.

5 When does offering people more make them want less?

The retirement fund analysis can be found in: Iyengar, S., G. Huberman and W. Jiang (2004), 'How much choice is too much?: contributions to 401(k) retirement plans', in O. Mitchell and S. Utkus (eds), *Pension Design and Structure: New Lessons from Behavioural Finance*, Oxford University Press, pp. 83–96.

The jam choice study can be found in: Iyengar, S. S. and M. R. Lepper (2000), 'When choice is demotivating: can one desire too much of a good thing?', *Journal of Personality and Social Psychology*, 79: 995–1006.

For more on company decisions to reduce the number of alternatives they offer, see: Osnos, E. (1997), 'Too many choices? Firms cut back on new products', *Philadelphia Inquirer*, 27 September, pp. D1, D7.

For those interested in learning more about why offering more choices can have a paralysing or destructive effect on others, see: Schwartz, B. (2004), *The Paradox of Choice*, New York: Ecco.

6 When does a bonus become an onus?

The bonus gift boomeranging study can be found in: Raghubir, P. (2004), 'Free gift with purchase: promoting or discounting the brand?', *Journal of Consumer Psychology*, 14: 181–6.

7 How can a new superior product mean more sales of an inferior one?

Both the bread-maker example and the research presented in this chapter can be found in: Simonson, I. (1993), 'Get closer to your customers by understanding how they make choices', *California Management Review*, 35: 68–84.

8 Does fear persuade or does it paralyse?

The public health study can be found in: Leventhal, H., R. Singer and S. Jones (1965), 'Effects of fear and specificity of recommendation upon attitudes and behaviour', *Journal of Personality and Social Psychology*, 2: 20–29.

9 What can chess teach us about making persuasive moves?

The news article detailing the reaction in Iceland to Bobby Fischer can be found in: Smith-Spark, L. (2005), 'Fischer "put Iceland on the map"', 23 March, retrieved from http://news.bbc.co.uk/2/hi/europe/4102367.stm.

The Regan Coke can study can be found in: Regan, D. T. (1971), 'Effects of a favour and liking on compliance', *Journal of Experimental Social Psychology*, 7: 627–39.

10 Which office item can make your influence stick?

The Post-it note research can be found in: Garner, R. (2005), 'Post-It Note persuasion: a sticky influence', *Journal of Consumer Psychology*, 15: 230–37.

11 Why should restaurants ditch their baskets of mints?

The tipping study can be found in: Strohmetz, D. B., B. Rind, R. Fisher and M. Lynn (2002), 'Sweetening the till: the use of candy to increase restaurant tipping', *Journal of Applied Social Psychology*, 32: 300–309.

12 What's the pull of having no strings attached?

These hotel study data are from a manuscript currently being prepared to undergo the peer review process: Goldstein, N. J., R. B. Cialdini and V. Griskevicius (2007), 'Maximizing motivation to cooperate toward the fulfillment of a shared goal: initiation is everything'.

13 Do favours behave like bread or like wine?

The study examining the effect of time on favour value can be found in: Flynn, F. J. (2003), 'What have you done for me lately? Temporal adjustments to favour evaluations', *Organisational Behaviour and Human Decision Processes*, 91: 38–50.

14 How can a foot in the door lead to great strides?

Both the ugly billboard study and the home invasion study can be found in: Freedman, J. L. and S. C. Fraser (1966), 'Compliance without pressure: the foot-in-the-door technique', *Journal of Personality and Social Psychology*, 4: 195–203.

The sales expert advice can be found in: Green, F. (1965), 'The "foot-in-the-door" technique', *American Salesman*, 10: 14–16.

15 How can you become a Jedi master of social influence?

The labelling technique study involving voting can be found in: Tybout, A. M. and R. F. Yalch (1980), 'The effect of experience: a matter of salience?', *Journal of Consumer Research*, 6: 406–13.

The labelling technique study with children can be found in: Cialdini, R. B., N. Eisenberg, B. L. Green, K. Rhoads and R. Bator (1998), 'Undermining the undermining effect of reward on sustained interest: when unnecessary conditions are sufficient', *Journal of Applied Social Psychology*, 28: 249–63.

16 How can a simple question drastically increase support for you and your ideas?

The voting study can be found in: Greenwald, A. G., C. G. Carnot, R. Beach and B. Young (1987), 'Increasing voting behaviour by asking people if they expect to vote', *Journal of Applied Psychology*, 72: 315–18.

The story of Gordon Sinclair's Chicago restaurant can be found in Cialdini, R. B. (2001), *Influence: Science and Practice* (4th edn), Boston, MA: Allyn & Bacon.

17 What is the active ingredient in lasting commitments?

This sales goal passage is discussed in: Cialdini, R. B. (2001), *Influence: Science and Practice* (4th edn), Boston, MA: Allyn & Bacon.

The active/passive commitment study can be found in: Cioffi, D. and R. Garner (1996), 'On doing the decision: effects of active versus passive commitment and self-perception', *Personality and Social Psychology Bulletin*, 22: 133–44.

The reference to missed appointments can be found in a survey by DPP: Developing Patient Partnerships (UK Department of Health funded charity), August 2006.

18 How can you fight consistency with consistency?

The research examining how preference for consistency increases with age can be found in: Brown, S. L., T. Asher and R. B. Cialdini (2005), 'Evidence of a positive relationship between age and preference for consistency', *Journal of Research in Personality*, 39: 517–33.

19 What persuasion tip can you borrow from Benjamin Franklin?

The connection between Ben Franklin's strategy and persuasion is described extremely well in: Aronson, E., T. D. Wilson and R. M. Akert (2005), *Social Psychology* (5th edn), Englewood Cliffs, NJ: Prentice Hall.

The Ben Franklin quote can be found in: Franklin, B. (1900), *The Autobiography of Ben Franklin* (ed. J. Bigelow), Philadelphia, PA: Lippincott (originally published in 1868).

The study that tested the Benjamin Franklin effect can be found in: Jecker, J. and D. Landy (1969), 'Liking a person as a function of doing him a favour', *Human Relations*, 22: 371–8.

20 When can asking for a little go a long way?

The even-a-penny-will-help study can be found in: Cialdini, R. B. and D. A. Schroeder (1976), 'Increasing compliance by legitimizing paltry contributions: when even a penny helps', *Journal of Personality and Social Psychology*, 34: 599–604.

21 Start low or start high? Which will make people buy?

The eBay study can be found in: Ku, G., A. D. Galinsky and J. K. Murnigham (2006), 'Starting low but ending high: a reversal of the anchoring effect in auctions', *Journal of Personality and Social Psychology*, 90: 975–86.

22 How can you show off without being labelled a show-off?

The study on using others to legitimise ourselves can be found in: Pfeffer, J., C. T. Fong, R. B. Cialdini and R. R. Portnoy (2006), 'Overcoming the self-promotion dilemma: interpersonal attraction and extra help as a consequence of who sings one's praises', *Personality and Social Psychology Bulletin*, 32: 1362–74.

23 What's the hidden danger of being the brightest person in the room?

The groups versus individuals study can be found in: Laughlin, P. R., B. Bonner and A. Minor (2002), 'Groups perform better than the best individuals on letters-to-numbers problems', *Organisational Behaviour and Human Decision Processes*, 88: 605–20.

24 What can be learnt from captainitis?

More information on the Flight 90 disaster can be found at: www. time.com/time/magazine/article/0,9171,925270,00.html or www. airdisaster.com/special/special-af90.shtml.

The nurse obedience study can be found in: Hofling, C. K., E. Brotzman, S. Dalrymple, N. Graves and C. M. Pierce (1966), 'An experimental study of nurse–physician relationships', *Journal of Nervous and Mental Disease*, 141: 171–80.

25 How can the nature of group meetings lead to unnatural disasters?

For more on groupthink, see: Janis, I. L. (1983), *Groupthink: Psychological Studies of Policy Decisions and Fiascoes* (2nd edn), Boston, MA: Houghton Mifflin.

The source of the *Columbia* investigation transcript is: Langewiesche, W. (2003), 'Columbia's last flight', *Atlantic Monthly*, 292: 58–87.

26 Who is the better persuader? Devil's advocate or true dissenter?

The devil's advocate versus true dissenter study can be found in: Nemeth, C., K. Brown and J. Rogers (2001), 'Devil's advocate versus authentic dissent: stimulating quantity and quality', *European Journal of Social Psychology*, 31: 707–20.

The evidence that using a devil's advocate has the ability to strengthen majority members' confidence in their original position can be found in: Nemeth, C., J. Connell, J. Rogers and K. Brown (2001), 'Improving decision making by means of dissent', *Journal of Applied Social Psychology*, 31: 48–58.

27 When can the right way be the wrong way?

The firefighters' training research can be found in: Joung, W., B. Hesketh and A. Neal (2006), 'Using "war stories" to train for adaptive performance: is it better to learn from error or success?', *Applied Psychology: An International Review*, 55: 282–302.

28 What's the best way to turn a weakness into a strength?

The study demonstrating the effects of admitting weaknesses in law can be found in: Williams, K. D., M. Bourgeois and R. T. Croyle (1993), 'The effects of stealing thunder in criminal and civil trials', *Law and Human Behaviour*, 17: 597–609.

29 Which faults unlock people's vaults?

The small-but-cosy study can be found in: Bohner, G., S. Einwiller, H.-P. Erb and F. Siebler (2003), 'When small means comfortable: relations between product attributes in two-sided advertising', *Journal of Consumer Psychology*, 13: 454–63.

Another informative study on this topic can be found in: Pechmann, C. (1992), 'Predicting when two-sided ads will be more effective than one-sided ads: the role of correlational and correspondent inferences', *Journal of Marketing Research*, 29: 441–53.

30 When is it right to admit that you were wrong?

The research on admitting mistakes can be found in: Lee, F., C. Peterson and L. A. Tiedens (2004), 'Mea culpa: predicting stock prices from organisational attributions', *Personality and Social Psychology Bulletin*, 30: 1636–49.

31 When should you be pleased that the server is down?

The glitches study can be found in: Naquin, C. R. and T. R. Kurtzberg (2004), 'Human reactions to technological failure: how accidents rooted in technology vs. human error influence judgements of organisational accountability', *Organisational Behaviour and Human Decision Processes*, 93: 129–41.

The information on how much time the average UK citizen is delayed by technical problems comes from the National Statistics website, which can be found at: www.statistics.gov.uk.

32 How can similarities make a difference?

The name similarity study can be found in: Garner, R. (2005), 'Post-It Note persuasion: a sticky influence', *Journal of Consumer Psychology*, 15: 230–37.

33 When is your name your game?

The quotes from the American version of *The Office* are from the episode entitled 'The Coup'.

The research examining the effects of names on major life decisions, such as careers and locations, can be found in: Pelham, B. W., M. C. Mirenberg and J. T. Jones (2002), 'Why Susie sells seashells by the seashore: implicit egotism and major life decisions', *Journal of Personality and Social Psychology*, 82: 469–87.

The study showing that people are more likely to marry those with similar-sounding names can be found in: Jones, J. T., B. W. Pelham, M. Carvallo and M. C. Mirenberg (2004), 'How do I love three? Let me count the Js: implicit egotism and interpersonal attraction', *Journal of Personality and Social Psychology*, 87: 665–83.

The study examining the effects of people's names on consumer preferences can be found in: Brendl, M. C., A. Chattopadhyay, B. W. Pelham and M. Carvallo (2005), 'Name letter branding: valence transfers when product specific needs are active', *Journal of Consumer Research*, 32: 405–15.

34 What tip should we take from those who get them?

The tipping study can be found in: van Baaren. R. B., R. W. Holland , B. Steenaert and A. van Knippenberg (2003), 'Mimicry for money: behavioural consequences of imitation', *Journal of Experimental Social Psychology*, 39: 393–8.

The first posture-mirroring study can be found in: Chartrand, T. K. and J. A. Bargh (1999), 'The Chameleon effect: the perception–behaviour link and social interaction', *Journal of Personality and Social Psychology*, 76: 893–910.

The study examining the consequence of posture-mirroring in negotiations can be found in: Maddux, W. W., E. Mullen and A. D. Galinsky (in press), 'Chameleons bake bigger pies and take bigger pieces: strategic behavioural mimicry facilitates negotiation outcomes', *Journal of Experimental Social Psychology*.

35 What kind of smile can make the world smile back?

The smiling research can be found in: Grandey, A. A., G. M. Fisk, A. S. Mattila, K. J. Jansen and L. A. Sideman (2005), 'Is "service with a smile" enough? Authenticity of positive displays during service encounters', *Organisational Behaviour and Human Decision Processes*, 96: 38–55.

36 What can be learnt from the hoarding of tea towels?

For one source of information on how the rescheduling of the royal wedding influenced buying behaviour, see: Dear, P. (2005), 'Fans "panic buy" 8 April mementos', 5 April, retrieved from http://news.bbc.co.uk/2/hi/uk_news/4412347.stm.

The source of the Australian beef study is: Knishinsky, A. (1982), 'The effects of scarcity of material and exclusivity of information on industrial buyer perceived risk in provoking a purchase decision', Unpublished doctoral dissertation, Arizona State University, Tempe.

37 What can you gain from loss?

The opening quotation can be found in Greenwald, J. (1985), 'Coca-Cola's big fizzle', *Time*, 22 July, p. 48.

An excellent account of the New Coke debacle can be found in: Thomas, O. (1986), *The Real Coke, the Real Story*, New York: Random House. A different facet of it is also discussed in: Gladwell, M. (2005), *Blink: The power of thinking without thinking*, New York: Little, Brown and Co.

The original loss aversion work can be found in: Kahneman, D. and A. Tversky (1979), 'Prospect theory: an analysis of decision under risk', *Econometrica*, 47: 263–91.

The effects of loss aversion on stockholder behaviour are discussed more in depth in: Shell, G. R. (1999), *Bargaining for Advantage*, New York: Penguin.

Research demonstrating loss aversion in management-oriented decisions can be found in: Shelley, M. K. (1994), 'Gain/loss asymmetry in risky intertemporal choice', *Organisational Behaviour and Human Decision Processes*, 59: 124–59.

38 Which single word will strengthen your persuasion attempts?

The Xerox studies can be found in: Langer, E., A. Blank and B. Chanowitz (1978), 'The mindlessness of ostensibly thoughtful action: the role of "placebic" information in interpersonal interaction', *Journal of Personality and Social Psychology*, 36: 639–42.

The studies showing the power of generating reasons in favour of a position can be found in: Maio, G. R., J. M. Olson, L. Allen and M. M. Bernard (2001), 'Addressing discrepancies between values and behaviour: the motivating effect of reasons', *Journal of Experimental Social Psychology*, 37: 104–17.

39 When might asking for all the reasons be a mistake?

The BMW versus Mercedes study can be found in: Wänke, M., G. Bohner and A. Jurkowitsch (1997), 'There are many reasons to drive a BMW: does imagined ease of argument generation influence attitudes?', *Journal of Consumer Research*, 24: 170–77.

Two studies that support our advice on imagery are: Gregory, L. W., R. B. Cialdini and K. M. Carpentar (1982), 'Self-relevant scenarios as mediators of likelihood estimates and compliance: does imagining make it so?', *Journal of Personality and Social Psychology*, 43: 89–99; and Petrova, P. K. and R. B. Cialdini (2005), 'Fluency of consumption imagery and the backfire effects of imagery appeals', *Journal of Consumer Research*, 32: 442–52.

40 How can the simplicity of a name make it appear more valuable?

The stock-naming studies can be found in: Alter, A. L. and D. M. Oppenheimer (2006), 'Predicting short-term stock fluctuations by using processing fluency', *Proceedings of the National Academy of Sciences*, 103: 9369–72.

The source of the jargon-filled quote is: Moore, B. (2006), 'The towers of babble: the worst excesses of workplace jargon can leave one begging for a translator – and a return to plain English', 9 October, retrieved from www.nypost.com/seven/10092006/atwork/the_towers_of_babble_atwork_brian_moore.htm.

The research on the effects of using big words can be found in: Oppenheimer, D. M. (2006), 'Consequences of erudite vernacular utilized irrespective of necessity: problems with using long words needlessly', *Applied Cognitive Psychology*, 20: 139–56.

41 How can rhyme make your influence climb?

The rhyming research can be found in: McGlone, M. S. and J. Tofighbakhsh (2000), 'Birds of a feather flock conjointly: rhyme as reason in aphorisms', *Psychological Science*, 11: 424–8.

42 What can batting practice tell us about persuasion?

The contrast research can be found in: Tormala, Z. L. and R. E. Petty (2007), 'Contextual contrast and perceived knowledge:

exploring the implications for persuasion', *Journal of Experimental Social Psychology*, 43: 17–30.

43 How can you gain a head start in the quest for loyalty?

The car wash study can be found in: Nunes, J. C. and X. Dreze (2006), 'The endowed progress effect: how artificial advancement increases effort', *Journal of Consumer Research*, 32: 504–12.

44 What can a box of crayons teach us about persuasion?

The colour name research can be found in: Miller, E. G. and B. E. Kahn (2005), 'Shades of meaning: the effect of colour and flavour names on consumer choice', *Journal of Consumer Research*, 32: 86–92.

45 How can you package your message to ensure it keeps going, and going, and going?

One important source of information on consumers' confusion of Energizer versus Duracell is: Lipman, J. (1990), 'Too many think the bunny is Duracell's, not Eveready's', *Wall Street Journal*, 31 July, p. B1.

An excellent review of the research on the role of memory in advertising can be found in: Keller, K. L. (1991), 'Memory factors in advertising: the effect of retrieval cues on brand evaluations', in A. A. Mitchell (ed.), *Advertising Exposure, Memory, and Choice*, Mahwah, NJ: Erlbaum, pp. 11–48.

A more general review of the research on memory aids can be found in: Tulving, E. and D. M. Thompson (1973), 'Encoding specificity and retrieval processes in episodic memory', *Psychological Review*, 80: 352–73.

We have previously articulated our recommendations for public health campaigns in: Goldstein, N. J. and R. B. Cialdini (2007), 'Using social norms as a lever of social influence', in A. Pratkanis (ed.), *The Science of Social Influence: Advances and Future Progress*,

Philadelphia, PA: Psychology Press. The book is an excellent academic resource covering recent social influence research.

One study showing that alcohol can make persuasive messages more effective can be found in: Macdonald, T., G. Fong, M. Zanna & A. Matrineau (2000), 'Alcohol, myopia and condom use: Can alcohol intoxication be associated with more prudent behaviour?', *Journal of Personality and Social Psychology*, 78: 605–19.

46 What object can persuade people to reflect on their values?

The eyes research can be found in: Bateson, M., D. Nettle and G. Roberts (2006), 'Cues of being watched enhance cooperation in a real-world setting', *Biology Letters*, 2: 412–14.

The Halloween study examining the effect of a mirror can be found in: Beaman, A. L., B. Klentz, E. Diener and S. Svanum (1979), 'Self-awareness and transgression in children: two field studies', *Journal of Personality and Social Psychology*, 37: 1835–46.

The research on having people state their names can be found in: Diener, E., S. C. Fraser, A. L. Beaman and R. T. Kelem (1976), 'Effects of deindividuation variables on stealing among Halloween trick-or-treaters', *Journal of Personality and Social Psychology*, 33: 178–83.

For more discussion on the problems with surveillance, see: Cialdini, R. B., P. K. Petrova and N. J. Goldstein (2004), 'The hidden costs of organizational dishonesty', *Sloan Management Review*, 45: 67–73.

The littering research can be found in: Kallgren, C. A., R. R. Reno and R. B. Cialdini (2000), 'A focus theory of normative conduct: when norms do and do not affect behaviour', *Personality and Social Psychology Bulletin*, 26: 1002–12.

47 Does being sad make your negotiations bad?

The *Sex and the City* quotes are from the episode entitled 'The Domino Effect'.

The sadness research can be found in: Lerner, J. S., D. A. Small and G. Loewenstein (2004), 'Heart strings and purse strings: carryover effects of emotions on economic decisions', *Psychological Science*, 15: 337–41.

48 How can emotion put persuasion in motion?

The research on how emotions reduce people's ability to discriminate between the magnitude of numbers can be found in: Hsee, C. K. and Y. Rottenstreich (2004), 'Music, pandas, and muggers: on the affective psychology of value', *Journal of Experimental Psychology: General*, 133: 23–30.

49 What can make people believe everything they read?

The quote from the Chinese political prisoner can be found on page 23 in: Lifton, R. J. (1961), *Thought Reform and the Psychology of Totalism*, New York: Norton. We found this quote in: Gilbert, D. T. (1991), 'How mental systems believe', *American Psychologist*, 46: 107–19.

The research showing that people are inclined to believe others' claims when they are low on cognitive resources can be found in: Gilbert, D. T., D. S. Krull and P. S. Malone (1990), 'Unbelieving the unbelievable: some problems in the rejection of false information', *Journal of Personality and Social Psychology*, 59: 601–13; and Gilbert, D. T., R. W. Tafarodi and P. S. Malone (1993), 'You can't not believe everything you read', *Journal of Personality and Social Psychology*, 65: 221–33. Our title was inspired by the title of the latter paper.

For those interested in learning more about Gilbert's fascinating ideas and research on the topic of happiness, see: Gilbert, D. T. (2006), *Stumbling on Happiness*, New York: Knopf.

The research showing how disrupting people's ability to think can increase compliance can be found in: Davis B. P. and E. S. Knowles (1999), 'A disrupt-then-reframe technique of social influence', *Journal of Personality and Social Psychology*, 76: 192–9; and in: Knowles E. S. and J. A. Linn (in press), 'Approach-avoidance model of persuasion: alpha and omega strategies for change', in E. S. Knowles and J. A. Linn (eds), *Resistance and Persuasion*, Mahwah, NJ: Erlbaum.

50 Are tri-meth labs boosting your influence?

The caffeine research can be found in: Martin, P. Y., J. Laing, R. Martin and M. Mitchell (2005), 'Caffeine, cognition and persuasion: evidence for caffeine increasing the systematic processing of persuasive messages', *Journal of Applied Social Psychology*, 35: 160–82.

Influence in the 21st century

The source of the story and quotes about No E-mail Fridays can be found in: Horng, E. (2007), 'No e-mail Fridays transforms office', 10 March, retrieved from http://abcnews.go.com/WNT/story?id=2939232&page=1.

The research examining the differences between online and face-to-face negotiation can be found in: Morris, M., J. Nadler, T. Kurtzberg and L. Thompson (2002), 'Schmooze or lose: social friction and lubrication in e-mail negotiations', *Group Dynamics: Theory, Research, and Practice*, 6: 89–100.

The study examining the solution to the online negotiation difficulties can be found in: Moore, D. A., T. R. Kurtzberg, L. Thompson and M. Morris (1999), 'Long and short routes to success in electronically mediated negations: group affiliations and good vibrations', *Organisational Behaviour and Human Decision Processes*, 77: 22–43.

The online persuasion research involving gender can be found in: Guadagno, R. E. and R. B. Cialdini (2002), 'Online persuasion: an examination of gender differences in computer-mediated interpersonal influence', *Group Dynamics: Theory, Research, and Practice*, 6: 38–51.

The studies demonstrating our overconfidence in how well our e-communications are understood can be found in: Kruger, J., N. Epley, J. Parker and Z. Ng, 'Egocentrism over e-mail: can we communicate as well as we think?', *Journal of Personality and Social Psychology*, 89: 925–36.

The diffusion of responsibility study can be found in: Darley, J. M. and B. Latané (1968), 'Bystander intervention in emergencies: diffusion of responsibility', *Journal of Personality and Social Psychology*, 8: 377–83.

The research showing the benefits of displaying competitors' prices on a company's web page can be found in: Trifts, V. and G. Haubl (2003), 'Information availability and consumer preference: can online retailers benefit from providing access to competitor price information?', *Journal of Consumer Psychology*, 13: 149–59.

The subtle but powerful effects of background images on web pages can be found in: Mandel, N. and E. J. Johnson (2002), 'When web pages influence choice: effects of visual primes on experts and novices', *Journal of Consumer Research*, 29: 235–45.

The research on how culture affects management practices can be found in: Morris, M., J. Podolny and S. Ariel (2001), 'Culture, norms, and obligations: cross-national differences in patterns of interpersonal norms and felt obligations toward co-workers', in *The Practice of Social Influence in Multiple Cultures*, ed. W. Wosinska, D. Barrett, R. Cialdini and J. Reykowski, Mahwah, NJ: Lawrence Erlbaum, pp. 97–123.

The studies showing how advertisement effectiveness differs across cultures can be found in: Han, S. and S. Shavitt (1994), 'Persuasion and culture: advertising appeals in individualistic and collectivist societies', *Journal of Experimental Social Psychology*, 30: 326–50.

The Jack Nicklaus story, including quotes, can be found in: Ferguson, D. (2005), 'Grieving Nicklaus meets press', 7 March, retrieved from www.thegolfgazette.com/print.php?sid=2074.

The cross-cultural consistency research involving Americans and Asians can be found in: Petrova, P. K., R. B. Cialdini and S. J. Sills (in press), 'Consistency-based compliance across cultures', *Journal of Experimental Social Psychology*, 43: 104–11.

The cross-cultural consistency versus social proof research involving American and Polish participants can be found in: Cialdini, R. B., W. Wosinska, D. W. Barrett, J. Butner and M. Gornik-Durose (1999), 'Compliance with a request in two cultures: the differential influence of social proof and commitment/ consistency on collectivists and individualists', *Personality and Social Psychology Bulletin*, 25: 1242–53.

The answering machine study can be found in: Miyamoto, Y. and N. Schwarz (2006), 'When conveying a message may hurt the relationship: cultural differences in the difficulty of using an answering machine', *Journal of Experimental Social Psychology*, 42: 540–47.

The idea that people from collectivistic cultures tend to place a greater emphasis on the relational function of communication than do people from individualistic cultures is discussed in more depth in: Scollon, R. and S. W. Scollon (1995), *Intercultural Communication: A Discourse Approach*, Cambridge: Blackwell.

The research showing how Japanese listeners tend to provide more feedback can be found in: White, S. (1989), 'Backchannels across cultures: a study of Americans and Japanese', *Language in Society*, 18: 59–76.

Ethical influence

Readers can learn more about the UK petrol shortage of 2000 at: http://news.bbc.co.uk/2/hi/in_depth/world/2000/world_fuel_crisis/default.stm.

Acknowledgements

Yes! 50 Secrets from the Science of Persuasion is essentially a collection of insights from the fascinating science of social influence. We are extremely thankful to the myriad of scientists who conducted the research that we have described throughout the text. Without their work, Yes! wouldn't be a book; it'd be a pamphlet.

In creating *Yes!*, we've been fortunate to have access to another collection of insights – those of our colleagues, partners and students. In particular, we would like to thank Vladas Griskevicius, Leah Combs, Jennifer Ottolino, Miguel Prietto, Stuart Shoen and Chaundra Wong for reviewing and providing feedback on various chapters of the book in the early stages. Thanks also to Dan Norris, Nick Pope, Dil Sidhu, Brian Ahearn, Kathy Fragnoli, Christy Farnbauch, John Fisher and Tim Batchelor for offering their own examples of how they used the science of persuasion to good effect.

In addition, we would like to express our gratitude to Daniel Crewe, our editor at Profile Books, for his energy, enthusiasm for the book at all stages, and valuable suggestions from cover to cover.

We're also lucky enough to have Bobette Gordon, who made our lives so much easier at every turn, allowing us to concentrate on writing the book instead of worrying about the details surrounding it. Her hard work and dedication to the success of this project have been invaluable. We value highly and appreciate the continuing support and working partnership with both Gary Colleran and Anne Buckingham from our UK office. Finally, we are truly grateful to Jenessa Shapiro and Bernie Goldstein for their critical feedback on all aspects of the book and, even more importantly, for their unending support.

Noah J. Goldstein

Steve J. Martin

Robert B. Cialdini

Index